JAMES THE LORD'S BROTHER:

WHOSE SON WAS HE?

WHAT WAS HIS POSITION IN THE CHURCH?

AND

WHAT CONNECTION HAS THE SUBJECT WITH THE PROTESTANT EPISCOPAL CHURCH IN THE UNITED STATES?

BY

REV. CHAUNCEY W. FITCH, D.D.

RECTOR OF ST. JAMES'S CHURCH, PIQUA, O.

NEW YORK:

PUBLISHED BY DANIEL DANA, Jr.

381 BROADWAY.

1858.

RENNIE, LINDSAY & CO.,
Stereotypers and Electrotypers,
81, 83, and 85 Centre-street,
New York.

PREFACE.

THE author begs leave to introduce the following pages by an extract of a letter from the Bishop of Ohio, addressed to the Rev. Dr. A.:

REV. AND DEAR SIR:

I believe you know something of a Tractate which the Rev. Mr. Fitch, of Ohio, has written on "James, the Lord's brother." He has recently completed a full carrying out of the argument, and made, I think, a very conclusive proof that James was the son of Joseph and Mary, and really, literally the Lord's brother. It upsets the whole Mariolatry of Rome, and all her claims to supremacy through Peter. * * *

I believe it would be as good an article, in the Romish controversy, as we could publish.

Yours, affectionately,

C. P. McILVAINE.

CINCINNATI, January 19, 1857.

The "Tractate" here referred to was not originally designed to be an argument, though here called such, and by that title was published in one of our periodicals, with a commendatory introduction by Bishop Henshaw. It was simply an investigation of an important historical fact, which the Church had lost sight of for more than a thousand years. When the investigation began, the inquirer was not thinking of any argument on any subject. He was aiming solely—in the course of his parochial labors—by a thorough investigation to determine for himself, and the people committed to his charge, what was the meaning of the passage (Gal. i. 19), "Other of the Apostles saw I none, save James the Lord's brother."

The inquirer's reading had satisfied him that there was literally such a person, whilst nearly all the world, for hundreds of years, had said there was not. The few who obtained glimpses of the truth had not the patience to pursue their inquiries, or the boldness to confront the tradition of ages.

In this little work, now given to the public, the facts only were sought—the argument followed of itself.

The numerous Scripture references in the fore part of the treatise may be a hindrance to one who, in this fast age, would read rapidly; but they were necessary to the perfection of the work, that the careful reader might both verify the quotations, and, what is equally important, see that the facts are stated in their natural order. If these quotations are accurately made and correctly understood, and if there is truth in Scripture and history, then the subject here presented is as important as Bishop McIlvaine represents it to be, and this little book proves all he says it does. These consequences necessarily follow, if the fact is established that there was really such an Apostle as "James the Lord's brother."

The author has not aimed to say all that might be said on each topic; on the contrary, he has studied to condense the proofs into as small a space as possible—not to make a book for the library only, but for the people. He has therefore omitted a discussion of the different meanings of the word "till," and he has not enlarged on the singular fact that the Saviour transferred the care of His mother from His brethren, with whom she heretofore lived, to John. Many similar subjects might have been pursued further, if the author had aimed to say all that he *could*, rather than all that he *need.*

Whoever will read this treatise—without having his mind pledged to a theory beforehand, but is willing to believe what Scripture and history clearly teach—will find enough said to make every truth plain.

C. W. F.

St. James' Church Parsonage,
Piqua, Ohio, Nov. 13, 1858.

THE ARGUMENT.

JAMES THE LORD'S BROTHER.

"THEN after three years I went up to Jerusalem to see Peter, and abode with him fifteen days; but other of the Apostles saw I none, save James the Lord's brother."*

Who was James, the Lord's brother?

Dr. Neander says, "this is the most difficult question in the apostolic history, and cannot yet be considered as decided." The question is not difficult in itself, but made so by the unfortunate method in which men have pursued their inquiries. For some centuries past, they have begun by first assuming a theory to be true, and then have labored to prove it.

The Church of Rome long ago asserted that Mary, the mother of Christ, died a virgin, having no child but Jesus, and therefore concludes at once our Lord had no brother. James, the son of Alpheus, is meant by "the Lord's brother."

Others in later times, like Dr. Lardner, begin thus: "As there were but twelve Apostles, and James the

---

* Galatians, i. 18, 19.

Lord's brother is called an Apostle, therefore he must have been one of the twelve, and James, the son of Alpheus, is meant by 'the Lord's brother.' "

Both these classes of reasoners come to the same conclusion—" our Lord had no brother." They could not have come to any other, if the facts from which they started were true, "that Mary had no child but Jesus," and "there never were but twelve Apostles."

This present investigation is conducted on the inductive method. It begins with no theory, but brings together all the facts recorded in Scripture and the statements of early historians, arranges them in chronological order, and then draws the conclusions which they necessarily teach. By this natural and easy method we learn all the known facts, and these will make a theory for themselves.

This course of inquiry will bring out clearly these truths, well understood in early times. 1st. There was such a person as James, different from the two Apostles of that name. 2d. He was the son of Joseph and Mary, and in that sense the brother of our Lord. 3d. He is called an Apostle, though not one of the twelve. 4th. Though he came into the apostleship after the twelve, he was made by them the presiding Apostle in the Church.

These facts will be brought out in part first of this treatise; others equally important, relating to his position in the Church, will be established in part second.

The three Jameses mentioned in Scripture are clearly distinguished by the ancient historians, thus:

1. James the Great, son of Zebedee, brother of John, and one of the twelve.

2. James the Less, son of Alpheus, brother of Judas, also one of the twelve.

3. James the Just, son of Joseph, brother of our Lord, and not one of the twelve.

To prove these facts, I begin with the earliest mention of these three men in the Gospels, and trace them step by step to the end. (Matt. x. 2): "Now the names of the twelve Apostles are these: the first, Simon who is called Peter, and Andrew his brother; James the son of Zebedee, and John his brother; Philip and Bartholomew; Thomas, and Matthew the publican; James the son of Alpheus;* and Lebbeus,† whose surname was Thaddeus; Simon the Canaanite; and Judas Iscariot, who also betrayed Him." Here, in chapter tenth, we find the first two Jameses among the twelve Apostles. Let us follow on through the Scriptures, noting each fact in the order of time.

(Matt. xiii. 54): "And when He was come into His own country He taught them in their synagogue, insomuch that they were astonished, and said, Whence hath this man this wisdom and these mighty works? Is not this the carpenter's son, and is not His mother called Mary? and His brethren James, and Joses, and Simon, and Judas; and His sisters, are they not all with us?" Here is a distinct mention of the third James, known as the brother of Jesus, the carpenter's son, that is, the son of Joseph. He was not one of the twelve; for he was still remaining with the family at

---

* Alpheus is elsewhere written Cleophas, Cleopas, and Clopas. Compare Mark, xv. 40, and John, xix. 25.

† Lebbeus, or Thaddeus, is in Acts, i. 13, called Judas the brother of James.

Nazareth, with his mother, and brothers, and sisters, after the other two Jameses had been chosen and sent forth with the twelve Apostles, as was stated in chapter tenth.

The other three evangelists likewise tell us that this James, the brother of Jesus, was remaining at home with the family, not a follower nor a believer in Christ, till some time after the other two Jameses were ordained Apostles.

(Mark, iii. 14): "He ordained twelve that they should be with Him," and amongst them were "James the son of Zebedee, and James the son of Alpheus." After this (verse 21) He was so incessant in teaching that He had not so much time as to eat bread; "when His friends* heard of it they went out to lay hold on Him; for, they said, He is beside Himself." Then, in verse 31, He tells distinctly who these friends were. "There came then His brethren and His mother, and standing without sent unto Him, calling Him." These brethren who came up without and said, He is beside Himself, were not among the twelve Apostles listening within.

After this, we read (Mark, vi. 1), Jesus came into His own country, and they there said of Him (verse 3), "Is not this the carpenter, the son of Mary, the brother of James, and Joses, and Judas, and Simon; and are not his sisters here with us? But Jesus said

* Friends, οἱ παῤ αὐτου, "those with Him," that is, not friends or relatives in general scattered abroad, but those who lived with Him—which Mark explained to be His "brethren and His mother." We learn from this that up to about this time, Jesus with His mother and brothers (as well as sisters) composed one household.

unto them, A prophet is not without honor, but in his own country, and among his own kin, and in his own house."

John, as well as Mark, declares this same fact concerning the cousins (sons of Alpheus) and the brothers of Christ—that James and Judas, sons of Alpheus, were Apostles, whilst, as yet, His brothers remained unbelievers. John says (vi. 70), "Have I not chosen you twelve." Then after this (vii. 3), "His brethren said unto Him, Depart hence, and go into Judea, that thy disciples also may see the works which Thou doest; * * for neither did His brethren believe in Him." Since one of the brethren of Jesus was James, we conclude that there was a James, the brother of our Lord, who was not one of the twelve Apostles, and for some time after the Apostles were chosen, he was not a believer in Christ, whilst his cousin James, the son of Alpheus, was both a believer and an Apostle.

Why is this James called the Lord's brother? Rome says "our Lord had no brother—that His mother lived and died a virgin." This story of the perpetual virginity of Mary, as well as the story of her immaculate conception, which is more recent, has not a shadow of foundation in Scripture nor in early history; but is plainly repugnant to both.

Whilst Rome asserts that Jesus was not the *first*-born, but the *only*-born of Mary, the Scripture declares that He was "the *only*-begotten of the Father" (John, i. 14); "the *first*-born of his mother" (Matt. i. 25).

As in all things it behoved Him to be "made like unto His brethren," there was a propriety that He who was to be "tempted in all points as we are," "that He might be touched with a feeling of our infirmities," should sustain the relation of a brother, whilst He learned obedience as a son. "As the children are partakers of flesh and blood, He took part of the same." He was a *brother* as well as a *son*.

Mary His mother was not a nun, neither did she at the same time obey the vows of *celibacy* and *matrimony*. She was the wife of Joseph. In what sense and to what extent she was his wife is disclosed with singular precision—with a precision which some, perhaps, might think too exact for a refined taste to relish. But there was need of it.

Though betrothed and even married to Joseph, she continued a virgin till after the birth of her first-born son, but no longer. (Matt. i. 24): "Then Joseph took unto him his wife, and knew her not till (ἕως ὁυ, till when) she had brought forth her first-born son."

The Holy Spirit would seem to have dictated this peculiar sentence expressly to decide the question of Mary's virginity, and her exact relationship to Joseph —that he did not always continue her Platonic lover; but at a certain time became her *husband*, and because she had other sons by this husband, Jesus is called her *first*-born and not her *only* son.

Compare the two expressions: "I know not a man" (Luke, i. 34); and, "Joseph took unto him his wife, and knew her not till she had brought forth her first born son;" they mark the exact duration of Mary's virginity. She could say, "I know not a man," till after the birth of her first son; from that date she lived with Joseph as his wife: she died the mother of children, of whom Jesus was the first-born, and James, and Joses, and Simon, and Judas, with their sisters, were the others (Matt. xiii. 55).

Isaiah had prophesied (vii. 14), "A virgin shall conceive and bear a son, and shall call his name Immanuel: (Matt. i. 23.) St. Luke says, Gabriel was sent "to a virgin espoused to a man whose name was Joseph" (i. 27). But inasmuch as Mary was married to Joseph at the time of the birth of Jesus, lest the world should say that He was not born of a virgin, and therefore Jesus was not the Immanuel (God with us), St. Matthew shows that the prophecy was fulfilled in Him, because Joseph did not know his wife till after the birth of her first-born; therefore Jesus was born of a virgin. Matthew did not say that Joseph never knew his wife; but in saying that he knew her not till the birth of Christ, he showed that her virginity continued as long as there was any necessity for it—the Scripture was fulfilled. The word *till* has the same meaning here as in the following sentence: Ruth, after the death of her husband, went to live with Naomi, her mother-in-law, and lodged with her till her marriage with Boaz. We can discover no reason why Joseph and his wife should not henceforth live together as any other husband and wife, but every reason why they should. The mediatorial character of Christ could not be affected by the manner of his mother's life after He was born. Our further inquiry will show that she did not understand enough of the divine character and dignity of this child to induce her, for his sake, to remain a virgin all her married life. If she had known it all, neither she nor we can discover a reason for doing differently from what she did—living with her lawful husband as his lawful wife.

After the birth of her first son, Mary is never called a virgin, but often and always a mother (Luke, i. 27; Matt. xiii. 55; Mark, vi. 3). The term *Virgin Mary* is not applied to her in Scripture after the birth of Christ.

Mary lived with Joseph as his wife for years, and they moved together from place to place (Matt. ii. 14). "When Joseph arose he took the young child and his mother by night and departed into Egypt" (verse 21). "And he arose and took the young child and his mother, and came into the land of Israel" (Luke, ii. 48). When Jesus was twelve years old, and staid behind His parents in Jerusalem, His mother said unto Him, "Son, why hast thou thus dealt with us? Behold, thy father and I have sought thee sorrowing." Mary had now been living with Joseph publicly, as his wife, for twelve years, and Jesus was the reputed son of them both; therefore she said to Him, "thy father and I."

Not only does Mary here acknowledge herself to be the wife of Joseph, but she is declared to be the mother of children, both sons and daughters. The names of her sons are given: James, and Joses, and Simon, and Judas. These sons lived with her, and attended her wherever she went. (John, ii. 12): "He, Jesus, went down to Capernaum, He, and His mother, and His brethren." (Mark, iii. 21): "There came then His brethren and His mother, and, standing without, sent unto Him, calling Him." This looks much more as if these were the sons of the mother with whom they lived, and with whom they moved about, and with whom they felt a family interest in Jesus, their brother, than that they were the sons of Cleophas and Mary his wife, with whom they did not reside, though they were still living (Luke, xxiv. 18; John, xix. 25). If Cleophas and his wife were their parents, why did this whole family leave their father and mother, and live with their poor aunt?

Because they did not belong to Cleophas they did not live with him, and because they were the sons of the mother of Jesus, they are always found in her company and of her family.

And because the sons of Mary were the brothers of Jesus, our Lord is called "the brother of James" (Mark, vi. 3), and James is called "the Lord's brother" (Gal. i. 19); that is, mutually brothers to each other.

These two men, Jesus and James, are called brothers, because they were the sons of the same mother. In Ps. lxix. 8, 9, are these three plain prophecies of Christ (and Christ said, all things written in the Psalms concerning me must be fulfilled): "I am become a stranger unto my brethren, and an alien unto my mother's children" (לבני אמי, to the sons of my mother); "for the zeal of thy house hath eaten me up." (Verse 21): "They gave me also gall for my meat, and in my thirst they gave me vinegar to drink."

All this language is uttered by the same person, and all was fulfilled in one and the same person, and the evangelists tell us that it was Christ. (John, ii. 17): "Then the disciples remembered that it was written, For the zeal of thy house hath eaten me up." If this last half of the sentence refers to Christ, the first half does also, and it is Christ who says, "I am become an alien to my mother's children, for the zeal of thy house hath eaten me up."

Matthew says (xxvii. 34), "They gave Him vinegar to drink, mingled with gall." Here was fulfilled in Christ those other words, "they gave me also gall for my meat, and in my thirst they gave me vinegar to drink." But the same person who says this, says also, "I am become an alien to my mother's children." Mother never means aunt, in Hebrew or English. "The sons of my mother are my brothers," not my cousins. Though the word brethren sometimes is used loosely for cousins or other relatives, still if He to whom they gave the vinegar and gall had brothers who were the sons of his mother, they were the sons of Mary, therefore Mary, his mother, had sons. This does not apply to James the son of Alpheus, and Judas the brother of James—they were not the sons of his mother, neither did they treat Christ as a "stranger and an alien."

Christ, in this prophecy, having said, "I am become a stranger to my brethren," foreseeing that men would say, brethren sometimes means cousins, shuts out that interpretation by explaining it, לבני אמי, "to the sons of my mother." Jesus, therefore, to whom they gave gall and vinegar, had brothers, who were literally the sons of His mother.

These brethren, the sons of His mother, fulfilled the prophecy of treating Him as an alien when they said, "Depart hence and go into Judea, that thy disciples may see the works which thou doest," for they did not believe in Him (John, vii. 3). When they came to lay hold on Him, for they said He is beside Himself, "they spake against their brother—they slandered their own mother's son" (Ps. l. 20). They treated Him *strangely*, because they thought Him *over-zealous*.

Since Mary the mother of Jesus was the wife of Joseph, and had sons, and Jesus her first born had brothers, and one of them was James, and Jesus was the brother of James, we infer that James the Lord's brother was the son of Joseph and Mary.

Who James the Lord's brother was, is plain enough. There is no intimation in Scripture that Jesus had not brothers. On the contrary, we are told that He had, and we are told their names.

There is no intimation in Scripture that Mary was not the wife of Joseph—we are told that she was.

There is no intimation in Scripture that Mary remained a virgin after she brought forth her first son; on the contrary, we are told that after that her husband knew her.

There is no intimation in Scripture that Mary had not children; on the contrary, they are often spoken of as being in company with her.

There is no doctrine of Scripture which requires us to believe that Mary had not children.

There is no doctrine or fact of Scripture which is weakened by admitting the plain truth, that Mary had children, and our Lord a brother James.

Why, then, should this question be the most "difficult in the apostolic history," to those whose creed does not compel them to believe in the perpetual virginity of Mary, nor to limit the number of Apostles to the original twelve?

This argument is urged by some: "Why did Jesus on the cross commit his mother to John, the beloved disciple? Therefore, Jesus had no brother." Solomon says, "Go not into thy brother's house in the day of thy calamity, for better is a neighbor that is near than a brother far off." "There is a friend that sticketh closer than a brother." John was that friend. When all the disciples forsook Christ and fled (Matt. xxvi. 56), John followed Him into the judgment-hall, and up to the foot of the cross (John, xviii. 15; xix. 26). Nor brother, nor cousin even was near; only John was there to receive the sacred trust—Christ's legacy of love.

Whether those brethren of our Lord with whom His mother lived, and in whose company we always find her, were her sons or her nephews, why John took her to his own home would be as difficult for those to explain who say they were her nephews, as for those who say they were her sons. If changing her home from living with them prove that they were not her sons, it would prove as clearly that they were not her nephews.

Almost the entire body of modern commentators have been led astray by copying, one after another, without due investigation, the error of some one who observed, that Mary, the wife of Cleophas (John, xix. 25), is elsewhere called, the mother of James the Less and Joses and Judas (Mark, x. 40), and also that the brothers of Jesus were James and Joses and Simon and Judas, and then concluded hastily that all these were but one family.

But if *Mary* the wife of Joseph, and *her sister Mary*

the wife of Cleophas, were named *alike*, it is not impossible, nor even surprising, that they should have given like names to several of their sons. (I say *sons*; for we are not told that the wife of Cleophas had daughters, as the wife of Joseph had.) We know the attachment of the Jews to family names. So strong was it, that great difficulty was found in giving a new one to John, because none of His family was called by that name (Luke, i. 61). That both these sisters were called *Mary*, is striking proof that the family was partial to particular names.

That there were two sets of children of these two *Marys*, is proved conclusively by the fact that things are repeatedly said of the brothers of Christ which were not true of His cousins, and things are said of His cousins which were not true of His brothers.

It is said (John, vii. 5), "neither did His brethren believe in Him." This was not true of His cousins; for before this (John, vi. 67), two of His cousins, James the son of Alpheus, and Judas the brother of James, were believing Apostles. The cousins believed, whilst His brothers did not. The families then were distinct.

The children of these two families appear distinct again when the brothers and mother of our Lord came to Him as He was teaching; they stood without, whilst His believing cousins were among His disciples within (Mark, iii. 21, 31).

I have admitted that the children of Cleophas (Alpheus) were the cousins of Jesus, for if Mary the wife of Joseph, and Mary the wife of Cleophas, were sisters (John, xix. 25), then James the Less was cousin to our Lord, on the mother's side. If these two Marys were not sisters, or if Alpheus and Cleophas were not the same person, then was not James the Less even cousin to our Lord.* In any case, whether cousins or not, the sons of Alpheus who *did* believe in Christ were not those brothers who *did not* believe in Him. There were two families.

If Christ was without honor in His own house, He was not without honor in the house of Alpheus. When our Lord complained that He was without honor in His own country, and among His own kin, and in His own house, this did not mean the house of Alpheus and its inmates; for that house had honored Him highly by furnishing two of His twelve Apostles.

There was a house properly called His own house, its inmates were His own kin, and among them it is true that He was without honor. (Matt. xiii. 55): "Is not this the carpenter's son? Is not his mother called Mary, and his brethren (*ἀδελφοι*), James and Joses and Simon and Judas? and his sisters (*ἀδελφαι*), are they not all with us?" Here is a regularly constructed family, like that in any house, consisting of the carpenter† and his wife, with their sons and daughters. These were His own kin and in His own house, composing one family. These are those unbelieving brethren who went to lay hold on Him, and stood without, whilst His believing cousins were listening Apostles within. These were those brethren, the sons of His mother, whose treating Him as an alien He foretold and complained of. If they did not believe in Him,

---

* Eusebius says, Joseph and Cleophas were brothers (Book III. 11); this, in law, would make James the Less cousin to Jesus.

† The carpenter they had known as its head when living.

and thought Him a fanatic and beside Himself, it is easy to understand their motive in going with their mother to get their unfortunate brother out of the crowd, take Him home and look after Him.

That James and Judas, the cousins, should have become devoted Apostles before the brothers were fully convinced that Jesus was more than they had known Him from His childhood, is what we witness often. When a man rises, though gradually, to great distinction above his fellows, his early companions can hardly believe he deserves his fame. They say, "Why! I knew him when a boy at school." But Christ did not rise *gradually*. He did not reveal Himself the Son of God, till He came out at once, at the legal time of assuming the priestly office, "being about thirty years of age." John first proclaimed Him to be the Lamb of God, at His baptism. This was at Jordan, away from His own village. Those who heard John and followed Jesus were strangers to Him, Andrew, Simon, Philip, and Nathaniel (John, i. 38, 40, 41, 43, 45). Christ tells us that His ministry and miracles had been begun elsewhere than in Nazareth, where His family resided (Luke, iv. 16). He came to Nazareth, where He had been brought up (ver. 23), "and He said unto them, Ye will surely say unto me this proverb, 'Physician, heal thyself.' Whatsoever we have heard done in Capernaum, do also here in thy country." The neighbors of Jesus and His brothers knew nothing of His miracles and divine character till He had gained disciples by them abroad, and amongst them, James and Judas, His cousins (Mark, iii. 18), and these two now came with Christ from Capernaum to Nazareth (Mark, vi. 1). His miracles at Capernaum were heard of at His home with incredulity. As they of His own country, own kin, and in His own house had known Him only as the carpenter's son, "subject unto His parents," as His brothers and sisters were, they could not, at once, credit this new claim to divine power. His neighbors said, "Is not this the carpenter's son? Do we not know Him and the whole family—mother, brothers, sisters—all?" They were offended at Him—rose up and thrust Him out of the city (Luke, iv. 29). His mother and brothers were more charitable—they only said, "He is beside Himself," and went to lay hold on Him, take Him home, and take care of Him.

The mother, doubtless, was moved with maternal solicitude for her son thus endangering Himself; with the brothers, however, there was more than a fraternal feeling; there was a mingling of incredulity and family pride.

But as we proceed we shall find that the truth was at last forced upon the mind of that mother, who had observed "all those things in her heart," and upon those brothers, as it was on the mind of the Roman centurion who was convinced by what he saw of our Lord on the cross, and said, "Truly, this was the Son of God."

Our investigation, thus far, has brought out distinctly these facts:

1. Jesus Christ our Lord had brothers, who were the sons of His mother.

2. Our Lord had a brother James.

3. Joseph and Mary lived together as husband and wife, and Jesus is called her first-born son.

4. The mother and brothers of Christ appear to be living together as one family, going together to call Him out of the crowd and take Him home, as members of one family having a common interest.

5. Although our Lord had cousins, James and Judas, they were believing Apostles at the time it was said, " His brothers did not believe in Him."

Hence we conclude there was such a person as James the Lord's brother, being the son of Joseph and Mary, and he was not one of the twelve Apostles.

Having ascertained from the Gospels whose son James the Lord's brother was, let us follow his history through the Acts and the Epistles ; here we shall find him in a new character, as different as Paul the Apostle was different from Saul of Tarsus.

(Acts, i. 13) : " When they were come in they went into an upper room where abode both Peter, and James, and John, and Andrew, Philip, and Thomas, Bartholomew, and Matthew, James the son of Alpheus, and Simon Zelotes, and Judas the brother of James. These all continued with one accord in prayer and supplication, with the women, and Mary the mother of Jesus, and with His brethren."

Here, in addition to the eleven, but not belonging to the eleven, we find the brethren of our Lord among the believers. At what time the brethren of Christ became obedient to the faith, is not recorded in Scripture—nor is it material to this inquiry. It is enough to know that they were not of the twelve Apostles; but were at length found amongst the faithful.

We have seen that the brethren of Christ kept back from Him for a time, and did not go out and in with Him, beginning from the baptism of John. They consequently had not enjoyed so much of the personal instructions of Christ as the chosen twelve. Possibly it was to obviate this disadvantage, especially in the eyes of the Apostles, that James, who was to be so prominent afterwards, was, like Paul, favored with a special revelation. (1 Cor. xv. 5): "Christ, after His resurrection, was seen of Cephas, then of the twelve; after that He was seen of above five hundred brethren at once; * * after that He was seen of *James*, then of all the Apostles; and last of all He was seen of me [Paul] also." Here James is spoken of as a person distinct from the twelve. Neither James nor Paul saw the risen Lord till after the twelve, for neither of them belonged to that body.

Eusebius, to show that there were more disciples than the seventy and more Apostles than the twelve, cites this passage in Corinthians (B. I. 12)*: "'After that He was seen of *James.*' He is said to have been one of the seventy disciples of our Saviour,† and also one of *the Lord's brethren.* Lastly, when besides these there was a considerable number who were called Apostles, in imitation of the twelve, such as Paul himself was, he adds, saying: 'Afterwards He appeared to all the Apostles.'"

Eusebius understands Paul to mean, that after Christ had shown Himself to the twelve Apostles, He appeared

* The edition of Eusebius quoted is, Cambridge, 1683.

† St. Luke, who records the commissioning of the seventy (x. 1), says nothing afterwards inconsistent with James' being among them.

to all the Apostles besides the twelve. Then, to anticipate the question what other Apostles were there besides the twelve, he says, "such as Paul himself was—for there was a considerable number who were called Apostles." Eusebius is doubtless correct in his understanding of this passage in 1 Corinthians, xv. 5.

Valesius, the Roman commentator on Eusebius, has this note: "Many of the ancient writers affirm that James, the brother of our Lord, he that was ordained the first bishop of Jerusalem, was not of the number of the twelve Apostles. Indeed, Paul (1 Cor. xv. 7) seems to favor this opinion, when, reckoning up those to whom Christ appeared after His death, after he had named the twelve Apostles and five hundred others, says, 'After that He was seen of James.'"*

There were the same reasons for conceding a special revelation to Paul and James, apart from the other Apostles. Paul was a chosen vessel unto the Lord; but he had been a persecutor and a blasphemer, and when he essayed to join himself to the disciples, they were afraid of him, and would not believe that he was a disciple, till Barnabas took him to the Apostles, and showed them how he had seen the Lord in the way,

* Valesius, who wrote the commentary on Eusebius, was a learned Doctor of the Church of Rome, and when he states that many of the ancient writers and St. Paul affirm that James the Lord's brother was not one of the twelve, he knew that his Church declares that this James was not the Lord's brother, but the son of Alpheus and one of the twelve. He had no motive to make the statement, except to state an acknowledged truth. To show what are the teachings of Scripture and early history was one thing, and to show what are now the teachings of Rome quite another thing. Valesius, like a true son of his Church, in a note to Book II. ch. 1, states what are the teachings of Rome, as though he were bound to believe her.

and that He had spoken to him (Acts, ix. 26). His previous ignorance required special instructions, and his previous character clear credentials. James, also, who was destined to great prominence in the Church, having been long an unbeliever, required both instructions and credentials, both for his own information and his credit with the Church.

Having traced the history of James the Lord's brother through the period of his unbelief, in the Gospels, and his being found among the disciples in the Acts, we next find him recognized as an Apostle.

(Gal. i. 18): "Then three years after, I [Paul] went up to Jerusalem to see Peter, and abode with him fifteen days; but other of the Apostles saw I none, save James the Lord's brother." The epithet "Lord's brother" distinguishes this James from the brother of John and the brother of Jude (Matt. x. 2, and Luke, vi. 16).

The assertion that there never were but twelve Apostles, like the story of Mary's perpetual virginity, has no foundation in Scripture nor history. In the language of Eusebius (B. I. 12), "there were many more besides the twelve who were called Apostles, by way of imitation, of which sort Paul himself was one." Paul certainly was not one of the twelve, yet he vindicates his claim boldly (1 Cor. ix. 1): "Am I not an Apostle? Yes, verily, and not a whit behind the very chiefest." Other Apostles there were who were not of the original twelve. (Acts, i. 26): Matthias was numbered with the eleven Apostles. Barnabas also was another. (Acts, xiv. 14): "Which, when the Apostles Barnabas and Paul heard of." Silvanus and Timotheus also claim each the prerogatives of an Apostle. (1 Thess. i. 1): "Paul and Silvanus and Timotheus unto the Church of the Thessalonians:" (ch. ii. 6), "when we might have been burdensome as the Apostles of Christ." Here Paul and Silvanus and Timotheus claim alike to be Apostles.

So then, if James the Lord's brother is called an Apostle, that does not prove that he must have been one of the twelve, and consequently that he must have been James the Less, son of Alpheus—for Paul certainly was an Apostle, though not of the twelve—Barnabas was certainly an Apostle, and not one of the twelve. So James could be an Apostle without being one of the twelve. The number was not limited. "There were many besides the twelve who were called Apostles."

If we begin without any prejudice or theory, and follow, in the simplicity of truth-seekers, the leadings of Scripture and let in the light of history on our path, there is no difficulty in arriving at an answer to the question, "Who was James the Lord's brother?" But if our search is not for the truth, but to establish a preconceived creed, and we begin by saying, "our Lord never had a brother," or by saying, "there never were but twelve Apostles," I confess that there could not be a more difficult question. By such a course of reasoning both Scripture and history are thrown into utter confusion, and another thousand years would leave the question "still undecided."

Travellers who set out to find Niagara Falls, some

insisting upon starting from the head of the Missouri, others from the head of the Mississippi, others from the head of the Ohio river, may all meet at a common point on the lower Mississippi, but they will not there find Niagara Falls.

Having found James the Lord's brother to have been the son of Joseph and Mary—contrary to the general teaching of the present age—before examining his position in the Church, it may not be irrelevant to show, briefly as possible, in what light our investigations place Mary his mother.

To dispose of the brethren of our Lord and find a mother for them, a great variety of singular and visionary schemes have been invented, besides transferring them from their own house to that of Alpheus, making them the children of their uncle and aunt, with whom they did not reside, and only the nephews of their mother with whom they did reside. These inventions were all originally forced attempts to sanctify celibacy, and cast odium upon matrimony; as if it were not true that marriage is honorable in all, and to be held honorable in all (Heb. xiii. 4); as if woman had not been created expressly to be a help to man, because it was not good for him to be alone. Hence the labor to put the children of Mary out of the way, and convert her into a nun in the house and arms of her husband.

The persecutions to which early Christians were subjected made a single life less perplexing. Celibacy, which for a time St. Paul commended as expedient, though he said he had no commandment of the Lord

(1 Cor. vii. 25, 26), very soon was looked upon with reverence as a heavenly virtue, and for some as a Christian duty.

Illustrious men tried their ingenuity to account for Christ's having brothers without his mother's having sons. Origen and others suppose that Joseph was a widower, with these children when he married Mary. This would dispose of her children, if Scripture authority would justify it, but leave her still with her husband and this passage of St. Matt. (i. 25) undisposed of: "Joseph took unto him his wife, and knew her not till ——"

Theophylact and others disentangled the knotty question thus: "Cleophas dying childless, his brother Joseph marries his widow, and these brethren of Jesus were the children of Joseph by her, and in this roundabout way came to be called the Lord's brethren." But Cleophas was living after the resurrection (Luke, xxiv. 18; John, xix. 25. See the Greek). This would give Joseph the wife of his brother without taking from him his own (Matt. i. 25).

All these theories of the ancients admit of James the Lord's brother's being the son of Joseph, therefore not the son of Alpheus. Their object was not in the early ages to get rid of the third James, but believing that a chaste virgin was a holier being than a chaste wife, they could not believe that the mother of Christ could be the wife of man. Origen carried his ideas of the greater sanctity of the unmarried life so far, that misunderstanding that passage (Matt. xix. 12), he disqualified himself for matrimony for the greater glory of God.

Those persons in all ages whose ideas of celibacy agree with those of Origen, cannot believe that Mary was a wife and mother, though proved to them, and yet many with Origen, and all of his class, admit that the brethren of Jesus were the sons of Joseph, and not of Alpheus.

There are other such ingenious devices to get rid of the maternity of Mary for the greater honor of celibacy. Each device will dispose of one difficulty by getting into another.

But no device has yet been invented to get around these two facts: Mary was the wife of Joseph—he knew her as such; and the brothers of Jesus were the "sons of His mother," and they lived with their mother.

Mary the wife of Joseph, and mother of Jesus, and James, and Joses, and Simon, and Judas, did not lead the secluded life of a nun, nor did she die a virgin. If she had died both nun and virgin she would have deserved no more reverence than she now does for being both wife and mother as she was.

If any one would honor Mary let her not bury herself in a cloister, but follow Mary's example, for that is the advice of St. Paul (1 Tim. v. 14): "I will therefore that the younger women marry, bear children, guide the house." "If a virgin marry she hath not sinned" (1 Cor. vii. 28).

One who is a wife and a mother occupies the very position for which she was created; thus far she follows the example of Mary. If faithful in these relations and God blesses her with a "family like a flock" (Ps. cvii. 41), let her not regard them as proofs of guilt and shame, but prize them as her jewels. Let her not grieve to be like Sarah, Hannah, and Eunice, rather than like Jephthah's daughter. Let her bring up her Samuels and Timothies in the nurture and admonition of the Lord, and bless God for the honor He hath put upon her in making her to be the "joyful mother of children" (Ps. cxiii. 9).

As Mary the wife of Joseph, and mother of Jesus and James and Joses, is not to be reverenced for being ever virgin, which she was not; so it is as easily shown that there is no authority in Scripture for adoring her because she was the mother that she was; neither for any supposed efficacy in her intercession with Christ; nor for any merit on her part in being His mother; nor for the supposed purity of her birth; nor for any agency of hers in the redemption of the world; nor for her love and guardianship to men.

Though as the Son of man, Jesus was subject to His human parents; yet, as the Son of God, His mother's interference in the slightest degree with the work of His divine mission was ever studiously repelled by Him, and sometimes in a manner to excite our surprise, if we forget that He is the only Mediator between God and man (1 Tim. ii. 5), and His glory will He not give to another. The first intimation of this jealousy on the part of Christ, was when at the age of twelve years His mother reproved Him for staying behind—"Son, why hast thou thus dealt with us?" He replied, "How is it that ye sought me? Wist ye not that I must be about my Father's business?" This was above her comprehension, but "she kept all these sayings in her heart" (Luke, ii. 48, 51).

Then again at the marriage in Cana, when His mother said to Him, "They have no wine," intimating that she expected something from Him—as Herod desired to see some miracle—He replied, "Woman, what have I to do with thee?* Mine hour is not yet come" —meaning, "*woman*—He did not say, *mother*—woman, why do you dictate to me what I am to do?"

Again: Christ taught (Matt. xii. 47) that the relationship of flesh and blood gave no mortal, either brother or *mother*, the privilege of interfering with His work as the Messiah. "Then said one unto Him, Behold thy mother and thy brethren stand without, desiring to speak with thee. But He answered and said unto him that told Him, Who is my mother and who are my brethren? And He stretched forth His hand towards His disciples and said, Behold my mother and my brethren—for whosoever shall do the will of my Father which is in heaven, the same is my brother and *sister* and MOTHER."

The fact of being Christ's mother gave her no voice in His divine work, no control over His actions as the Son of God. It was always thus while she lived—we see no reason why it should be different now that she is dead.

---

* The expression Τί ἐμοὶ καὶ σοὶ, "what have I to do with thee," occurs often in the Septuagint, and there its meaning is easily ascertained. (2 Sam. xix. 22): Abishai son of Zeruiah said to David, Shall not Shimei be put to death for this? David said, "What have I to do with you, ye sons of Zeruiah?" Meaning, "Why do you sons of Zeruiah dictate to me the king what I ought to do?"

Though to a superficial Greek scholar it appears as if our translators had not accurately rendered the passage in John, ii. 4, a careful investigation of every place where the expression (Τί ἐμοὶ καὶ σοὶ) occurs, will show that it always has a reproving meaning, like the one here given.

Again we read (Luke, xi. 27), "It came to pass as He spake these things, that a certain woman of the company lifted up her voice and said unto Him, Blessed is the womb that bare thee and the paps which thou hast sucked! But He said, Yea, rather blessed are they which hear the word of God and keep it." There is then a blessedness greater than being the mother of Christ. We have his own authority for saying, that to be an obedient believer in Christ is the highest honor which any mortal could attain.

Of Mary we have greater things to say, than that she was the mother of our Lord. As the Holy Ghost said to her by the mouth of Elizabeth, "Blessed is she that believed" (Luke, i. 45).

After the ascension of Christ, during the lifetime of the Apostles, there was the same guarded caution against the undue exaltation of Mary. Although James the Lord's brother was honored by the Church above all the Apostles—for there was no danger that men would make a divinity of him—the only mention made of his mother is in this single passage (Acts, i. 14): "All these Apostles continued with one accord in prayer and supplication with the women, and *Mary the mother of Jesus*, and with His brethren."

This was as little as could have been said, to let the world know that Mary still lived and was one amongst the believers. But it was as much as it was safe to say, in a world so prone to love and serve the creature more than the Creator.

As the burial-place of Moses was concealed lest men should deify his relics, so Mary's later history and her end have been shrouded in silence—put entirely out of sight by the sacred writers so that not a bone was preserved to be recognized and worshipped.

If the attempt had been made by after ages to pay undue honors to James the Lord's brother, something like encouragement might have been found for it in the deference paid to him by the Apostles; but not the least shadow of encouragement can be found in the language or actions of Christ or His Apostles for offering adoration or prayers to His mother.

The great plan of our redemption was not devised by Mary's wisdom, nor did her zeal or love aid to carry it out. When the angel announced to her that she was to be the mother of Immanuel, she was taken by surprise, she "was troubled at his word, and cast in her mind what manner of salutation this should be" (Luke, i. 29). The angel said: "Hail (κεχαριτωμένη) thou, on whom a great favor has been conferred." That she should be the mother of the Messiah was a favor conferred by the Father on her, and not an obligation conferred by her on mankind. She confessed this (Luke, i. 49): "He that is mighty hath done great things for me." In like manner St. Paul said of himself (Eph. iii. 8): "Unto me, who am less than the least of all saints, is this grace given that I should preach among the Gentiles the unsearchable riches of Christ." We congratulate St. Paul for the grace shown to him, but we do not adore him for it. The Gospel which he preached was not his own.

As Mary did not originate the plan of redemption, and was merely the passive agent of the Father in giving birth to the Saviour, so in all His after-life she bore no part in atoning for the sins of the world. It was

Christ only who gave Himself a ransom. "He trod the wine-press alone, and of the people there was none with Him." He is the only mediator between God and man. His is the only name under heaven given among men, whereby we must be saved. It is the blood of Christ, and Christ alone, that cleanseth from all sin. Mary did not aid Him in making the atonement; she may not divide the honor with Him.

As it was not the wisdom and forethought of Mary that provided redemption, so neither was it her love to ruined man. It was God who so loved the world; it was God who gave His only-begotten Son, that whosoever believeth in Him should not perish. It was not the love of Mary, but the love of Christ that made the atonement.

Inasmuch as the Son of God was to be born of a woman (Gal. iv. 4), and not of an angel, that the honor of being that woman was given to Mary, a mortal like ourselves, the daughter of human parents, like any other daughter of Adam, we may with all nations call her "blessed." But our undivided worship we give, as most bounden, to the Triune God who created, redeemed, and sanctifieth us.

Since the mother of Christ was born of human parents like any other child of man, and was the wife of a mortal husband like any other wife, and was the mother of children like any other mother in Israel, we conclude that she partook of our common humanity.

Yet if she had been more than human, not only immaculate but a spotless angel, still the Christian who should fall down before her feet to worship would be rebuked by her, as was John by the angel: "See thou do it not; worship God" (Rev. xxii. 8, 9).

Having ascertained the parentage of James the Lord's brother, and shown in what light Scripture presents Mary his mother, I come now to notice the particulars in the life of James, from which all *his* importance in the history of the Church is derived.

On further inquiry we find that James the Just, the Lord's brother, though not one of the twelve Apostles, was the first Bishop of Jerusalem, and had precedence assigned him before all the Apostles, and presided in the first council of the Church, composed of Apostles, Elders, and Brethren.

It might have been expected that when the Church was met in council, as it was a deliberative body, and must have a head, the post of honor would have been assigned to one of the three whom the Lord in His lifetime had distinguished above the others, either to Peter or James or John (Matt. xvii. 1; xxvi. 7). But, as if to show how the first shall be last and the last first, the highly honored James, son of Zebedee, was early put to death. (Acts, xii. 1): "Now about that time Herod the king * * killed James the brother of John with the sword." The James, therefore, whom we find so prominent in Scripture afterwards, was not the brother of John. St. Paul says he was the "brother of our Lord" (Gal. i. 19).

How the Lord's brother, who came late into the Apostleship, came to be placed in honor above all the Church, is thus explained by Eusebius (B. II. 1): "This

James also, who is termed the brother of the Lord, because he is called the son of Joseph * * this James, whom for his eminent virtues the ancients surnamed 'the Just,' was, as they relate, the first that had received the Episcopal seat of the Church at Jerusalem delivered to him." So Clemens affirms, in the 6th Book of his Institutions: for he says, that after the ascension of our Saviour, Peter, James, and John, although our Lord had preferred them before the rest, did not contend for the dignity, but chose James the Just bishop of Jerusalem.* Paul makes mention of this James the Just, writing thus: "other of the Apostles saw I none, save James the Lord's brother."

This one paragraph writes out in full the name and surname, the family, titles, and honors of the man whose history we followed through the Scriptures. Here they are: "James"—"the Just"—"the son of Joseph"—"the brother of the Lord"—"the first Bishop of Jerusalem"—"placed by Peter, James, and John in dignity above themselves." He is not James the Less, Eusebius is careful to tell us, but James the Just. He is not the son of Alpheus, but the son of Joseph; not the brother of Judas, but the brother of our Lord.

To prove the distinction between these two men, did not necessarily involve the question, Who was the mother of the Lord's brother? What follows is independent of that question.

Writers who find the subject of James the Lord's

---

* Only the day before the crucifixion there was a contention among these disciples, which should be accounted the greatest! Christ taught them a lesson of humility (Luke, xxii. 24). See here how well they profited by it.

brother "the most difficult in the Apostolic history," being unable to ascertain whose son he was, find no difficulty in determining that he was the head of the Church in Jerusalem, whoever may have been his parents. Dr. Lardner, who could not tell who he was, says, that "the appointment of James to reside at Jerusalem and superintend the Church there, was made soon after the martyrdom of Stephen;" and in support of this opinion, observes: "After the choice of the seven deacons, every thing said of James implies his presiding in the Church in Jerusalem." Several of these examples thus alluded to by Dr. Lardner are quoted and commented on by Dr. Adam Clarke. Speaking of the Council of Jerusalem, Dr. Clarke says:—In the time of this council, Paul communicated the Gospel which he preached among the Gentiles to three of the Apostles, whom he calls "pillars," and tells us that when they perceived the inspiration and miraculous powers which he possessed, they gave him the right hands of fellowship, mentioning James first. (Gal. ii. 9): "And when James, Cephas, and John, who seemed to be pillars, perceived the grace which was given unto me, they gave to me and Barnabas the right hands of fellowship." This implies that James, whom in the first chapter he had called the Lord's brother, was not only an Apostle, but the presiding Apostle at Jerusalem. In the same chapter Paul, giving an account of what had happened after the council, says (ver. 11): "When Peter was come to Antioch I withstood him to the face, because he was to be blamed, for before that certain came from James he did eat with the Gentiles, but when they were come he withdrew and separated himself, fearing them who were of the circumcision." This shows that James resided at Jerusalem, and presided in the Church there, and was greatly respected by the Jewish believers. The same circumstance appears from Acts, xxi. 18, when giving an account of Paul's journey to Jerusalem with the collection for the saints in Judea. Luke says: "Paul went in with us unto James, and all the elders were present." Further, the respect in which James was held by the Apostles, appears by two facts recorded by Luke. The first is, when Paul came to Jerusalem, three years after his conversion, Barnabas took him and brought him to Peter and James as the chief Apostles (Acts, ix. 27, Gal. i. 19). The second fact is, after Peter was miraculously delivered out of prison, he said to those in the house of Mary, "Go show these things unto James."*

Dr. Clarke speaks of the "great respect in which James was held at Jerusalem." But there was something more than personal respect, and it was not confined to Jerusalem. His controlling influence extended to persons and places where we should not have looked for it. Observe how the boldest Apostle felt it (Gal. ii. 11): "When Peter was come to Antioch I withstood him to the face, because he was to be blamed, for before certain came from James he did eat with the Gentiles, but when they were come he withdrew and separated himself." Yet this is that Peter who had said to Cornelius, "God hath shown me that I should not call any man common or unclean;" and

---

* Clarke's Preface to the Epistle of James.

when called to account for it at Jerusalem and accused thus, "Thou didst go in to men uncircumcised and didst eat with them," he manfully defended himself and said, "What was I, that I could withstand God?" But now at Antioch, eating with Gentile Christians, as he had claimed the liberty of doing, as soon as the messengers from James, who "was zealous for the law," appeared, he withdrew, he yielded, not because he was convinced. He knew that he was right, for the Holy Ghost had otherwise commanded (Acts, x. 28).

Such deference did Peter pay to James! If, on the contrary, Peter had been residing at Rome, and had sent such a message to James, and James had instantly turned around against his own better judgment and done at Peter's bidding things for which he deserved to be blamed, what an argument it would have been to prove the supremacy of Peter, and a supreme power lodged at Rome! But the potent word came from Jerusalem, and not from Rome; it came from James to Peter.

If we are surprised at the compliance (shall I say *blamable compliance?*) of Peter with the wishes of James, we are not less so at that which Paul himself exhibited. He could withstand Peter to his face, but bowed in silence to the first word of James. Thus he wrote to the Galatians (ii. 4): "False brethren came in privily to spy out our liberty which we have in Christ Jesus, that they might bring us into bondage, to whom we gave place by subjection, no not for an hour;" (v. 1)—"Stand fast, therefore, in the liberty wherewith Christ hath made us free, and be not entangled again with the yoke of bondage. Behold I, Paul, say unto you, that if ye be circumcised, Christ shall profit you nothing."

Let us see how this champion for religious liberty, who could expostulate with Peter and the Galatians, stands a mute, obedient listener in the presence of James.

Luke writes (Acts, xxi. 17): "When we were come to Jerusalem the brethren received us gladly, and the day following Paul went in with us unto James, and all the elders were present;" (v. 20)—"And they said unto him, Thou seest, brother, how many thousands of Jews there are which believe, and they are all zealous of the law, and they are informed of thee that thou teachest all the Jews which are among the Gentiles to forsake Moses, saying they ought not to circumcise their children, neither to walk after the customs. * * Do therefore this that we say unto thee. We have four men which have a vow on them: take them and purify thyself with them, and be at charges with them, that they may shave their heads, and all may know that those things whereof they are informed concerning thee are nothing." Then Paul took the men "and did as required," though it cost him his liberty and nearly his life. Such deference did Paul pay to James!

On questions of expediency, not affecting the truth of the Gospel, Paul and Barnabas might differ, and neither yield to the other (Acts, xv. 27). Paul did not hesitate to speak his mind to Peter: but however much Paul or Peter may differ from James, and they be in the right, when once James has spoken, never is there a word in reply! They let him overrule their judgment and control their liberty.

The deference paid to James was not limited to individual examples. It was conceded to him by the whole Church. This brings me to the most important chapter in the life of the Lord's brother. To this I invite the reader's minute attention.

A question arose at Antioch which required the authoritative decision of the Church catholic. Where shall they meet, and who shall preside? The Apostolic commission points out the place. (Luke, xxiv. 47): "Repentance and remission of sins should be preached in His name among all nations, *beginning at Jerusalem.*" Accordingly at Jerusalem, the mother Church, the council was held; and James the Lord's brother we find presiding.

(Acts, xv. 2): "They at Antioch determined that Paul and Barnabas and certain other of them should go up to Jerusalem unto the Apostles and Elders about this question." (Ver. 6): And the Apostles and Elders came together to consider of this matter. And when there had been much disputing, Peter rose up and said unto them, Men and brethren, ye know how that a good while ago God made choice among us that the Gentiles by my mouth should hear the word of the Gospel and believe" * * (Ver. 21): "Then all the multitude kept silence and gave audience to Barnabas and Paul, declaring what miracles and wonders God had wrought among the Gentiles by them. And after they had held their peace, James answered, saying, Men and brethren, hearken unto me. Simeon hath declared how God at the first did visit the Gentiles to take out of them a people for His name, and to this agree the words of the prophets * *; wherefore, *my sentence is* (εγω κρινω, *I decide*), that we trouble not them which from among the Gentiles are turned to God, but that we write unto them" so and so. (Ver. 23): And "they wrote letters after this manner: The Apostles and Elders and Brethren send greeting unto the brethren which are of the Gentiles in Antioch and Syria and Cilicia * * It seemed good to the Holy Ghost and to us"—then follows the decree, copied from the sentence pronounced by James. (xvi. 4): "As Paul and Silas went through the cities they delivered them the decrees for to keep, which were ordained of the Apostles and Elders which were at Jerusalem. And so were the churches established in the faith."

Every fact recorded in this transaction tells on the history of the Church, and goes to establish a principle in its constitution and government.

We notice, to begin with, that same deference paid to James by the entire council of Apostles, Elders, and Brethren, which at all times was paid by individual Apostles. When James speaks they say no more, but uniformly act as he says.

Here Peter, in whom God wrought effectually to the Apostleship of the circumcision (Gal. ii. 8), rises up, as any other speaker in the discussion, and states what facts his experience furnished, to aid the council to a decision; and Barnabas did the same, furnishing facts; and Paul (who was mighty towards the Gentiles) related his experience in the ministry bearing on the subject. Finally, when they were all through, and all held their peace, James demands their attention, sums up the whole, gives his *decision*, and prescribes or suggests the form of the decree which was adopted by the council, and sent out in the name of the "Apostles, Elders, and Brethren."

If we look for the presiding officer in this council, there is no difficulty in finding him. It is James.

If the question is asked, Why did James preside? St. Chrysostom says, "It was because he was Bishop of Jerusalem."

The other Apostles, so far as their history is developed in the "Acts," were itinerating and crossing each other's path without any fixed residence; but James from the first was stationed at Jerusalem, and whenever business called the other Apostles to that city they find him there, from the time that Peter was delivered out of prison till Paul was cast into prison; and they always treat him with that respect customary when coming within the jurisdiction of one placed in high authority.

In truth, the deference paid to James, especially by *Peter* and *Paul*, was sometimes carried to an extent which we, at this distance of time, are not able to account for.

If the Church at Jerusalem had continued till now, and her Bishops had been continued on in uninterrupted succession, and her present Bishop were claiming an authority over all others by virtue of being the successor of him who was Bishop of the mother Church —who was placed by Peter, James, and John at their head (Eusebius, B. II. 1), and whose supremacy was proved by his presiding in the Apostolic Council, it might perhaps give the world trouble to disprove his claim. It might, then, be an important inquiry, "By what right did James, the Bishop of Jerusalem, preside in the Apostolic Council? Was it the mother Church which gave her Bishop precedence? or would James have presided, in his own right, if the assembling had been in any other place?"

But, providentially, for the present, it is enough for us to know that the only Apostolic Council, whose decrees speak to us with the authority of inspiration, was held at *Jerusalem*, and not at *Rome*, and the presiding Apostle was James, and not Peter.

The claim to supremacy over all the world is not made by the only Church which could claim to be the mother of us all, nor by a Bishop claiming to inherit the right through James, the only Apostle who was the acknowledged presiding head of all orders in the Church.

This fifteenth chapter of Acts is pregnant with facts respecting the original constitution of the Church. It teaches—

1st. That all local Churches, as of Antioch, Syria, Cilicia, and Jerusalem, were not independent of each other, each congregation being a perfect Church in itself—they were individually members of that Church of Christ which was one body.

2d. All the branches of the one Church were established in the common faith and common discipline by the decrees of a common Council acting for all.

3d. Jerusalem was the centre of the Church catholic; Rome was not.

4th. The Bishop of Jerusalem, and not the Bishop of Rome, presided in this council, whose decrees were for all Churches.

5th. The presiding Bishop in this council, which

passed decrees which "seemed good to the Holy Ghost," and which established the Churches everywhere in the faith, was James, and not Peter.

6th. Peter was not absent from this council; but was present, as any other member, taking part in the debate with Barnabas and Paul.

7th. The presiding Apostle in this inspired council, where Peter and Barnabas and Paul were speakers, was not one of the twelve Apostles; but James the Lord's brother, who was not one of the twelve.

8th. Since James the Just, the Lord's brother, who was not one of the twelve, presided in this great council, therefore the Apostolic office was continued in the Church in such full force, that an Apostle, who came in after the twelve, presided over Apostles, Elders, and Brethren.

These important conclusions also necessarily follow:

1st. James being the presiding Apostle in the Church catholic, Peter was not.

2d. If Peter was not supreme in the Church, no one after him could claim supremacy, by virtue of being the successor of Peter.

3d. If Jerusalem was the city and Church to which they went for a decision on questions of doctrine and discipline, then Rome was not the mother and mistress of Churches.

We notice also this significant fact: of the four Apostles mentioned by name as participating in this council, three—James, Barnabas, and Paul—were not of the original twelve.

That there were in this council, approved of by the Holy Ghost, three Apostles who were not of the original number ordained in the lifetime of our Lord, and that James, who was not of that twelve, presided over all, teaches that the Apostolic office was extended to others besides the twelve, and that in rank and official power these later Apostles were in no degree inferior to the first. Though James was one of the later Apostles, yet, as president of the council, his position was superior to that of Peter, who was but a common member, standing on a common level with Barnabas and Paul, who came into the Apostleship later than he.*

As I showed in the first part of this treatise, from the Gospels, the relation which James sustained to Christ—that he was the Lord's brother, being the son of Joseph and Mary—so here have I shown, from the Acts and Epistles, the relation which he sustained to the Church, —that he was the Apostle who resided permanently the Bishop of Jerusalem, and was the presiding Apostle in the Church when convened in council.

If the Scriptures are plain respecting the existence of James, who he was, and what his standing in the Church, equally so are the ancient historians.

Eusebius says (B. II. 23), "Hegesippus, being one of those who were of the first succession after the Apos-

* I would call the reader's attention to the fact that the constituents of the General Convention of the Protestant Episcopal Church in the United States are the same as composed the Apostolic Council in Jerusalem, viz., Apostles, Elders, and Brethren, or, in modern dialect, Bishops, Presbyters, and Laymen. Though there were deacons both then and now, they do not appear in council or convention.—[See Constitution of the Protestant Episcopal Church in the United States.]

tles, does, in the fifth book of his Commentaries, expressly relate these things concerning this James: 'James the brother of our Lord, together with the Apostles, undertook the government of the Church—that James who was surnamed "the Just" by all, even from the times of our Lord; for many were called by the name of James.' "

What pains are here taken to be very exact. Because, as Eusebius and Hegesippus say, there were many of the name of James, they are careful to distinguish him who, aided by the Apostles, undertook the government of the Church, from all others with whom he might be confounded. They call him "James the Just," to distinguish him from "James the Less." James the Just, Eusebius had before said, was the son of Joseph (B. II. 1). James the Less was the son of Cleophas (compare Mark, xv. 40, and John, xix. 25). They call him likewise the brother of our Lord, to distinguish him from the brother of John and the brother of Judas. They describe him, and give a full definition of him, his family, his residence and office, with sufficient plainness; but then the surname *the Just* distinguishes him, by one word, from James the Great and James the Less. These two were amongst the twelve Apostles. James the Just was neither of these.

Respecting the death of this James the Lord's brother, Clement, quoted by Eusebius (B. II. 1 and 23), says, "He was martyred by the Jews, being thrown from a battlement of the temple; and that not killing him, he was beaten to death by a fuller's club."

The question, who was "James the Lord's brother," might seem to be fully answered, if we conclude with his death, but we gain additional light by following on, and seeing how he was related to his successor.*

Eusebius says (B. III. 11), "After the martyrdom of James and the destruction of Jerusalem, which followed thereupon, report goes that the Apostles and Disciples of our Lord who were yet alive met together in the same place, together with the kinsmen of our Lord, according to the flesh, for many of them hitherto survived, and that all these held a consultation in common—who should be adjudged worthy to succeed James; and moreover that all, with one consent, approved of Simeon the son of Cleophas—of whom the history of the Gospel makes mention—to be worthy of the Episcopal seat there; which Simeon, as they say, was cousin (ανεψιον) to our Saviour, for Hegesippus relates that Cleophas was the brother of Joseph."†

Observe here that Simeon the son of Cleophas is called the "cousin of our Saviour," whilst James is never called the cousin, but always the brother, both in Scripture and history. But if James and Simeon had been both sons of Cleophas, as some say, they would have been brothers to each other, and both would have stood in the same relation to Christ, in the eye of the law: the one would not have been his brother and the other his cousin.

If Eusebius had understood James, the presiding Apostle at Jerusalem, to be the son of Cleophas, as he

---

* To what extent and in what sense the Apostles had successors, will be examined hereafter in these pages.

†

of Mai

side also.

says Simeon was, he would have said at once, "James was succeeded by his brother Simeon;" and he would have called Simeon the brother, not the cousin of our Saviour, for Simeon would have been as much entitled to be called the Lord's brother as his brother James was.

When the word *αδελφος*, brother, is applied to James, and *ανεψιος*, cousin, is applied to Simeon, they manifestly are used to express the exact relationship which these two men sustained to our Saviour. And inasmuch as the term cousin is never applied to James, and brother is never applied to Simeon, it is evident that Joseph and Simeon were differently related to Christ: the one was—on the mother's side literally, on the father's side legally—the Lord's brother; the other was His cousin.

As James and Simeon are not anywhere called brothers, we conclude it is because they were not brothers: but Simeon was the son of Cleophas; James, therefore, was not the son of Cleophas. The relationship betwixt James and his successor was plainly this:

James was the son Joseph, and brother to our Lord.

Simeon was the son of Cleophas, and cousin to our Lord.

James the Lord's brother is sufficiently distinguished from the son of Cleophas, from all the other Apostles, and from all other men in the world, by every name, epithet, and characteristic which can distinguish one man from another.

"Who was James the Lord's brother?" is no more doubtful than, "Who was the father of Zebedee's children?" Yet for more than a thousand years the very existence of this eminent and strongly marked man has been denied.

Though for a few centuries his name has been blotted out from the records of man, it will not be found blotted out of the Book of Life.

The facts gleaned from Scripture and history both coincide, and place before us with perfect distinctness these three:

1st. James the Great, son of Zebedee, brother of John, and one of the twelve, and early beheaded.

2d. James the Less, son of Alpheus—elsewhere called Cleophas—brother of Judas, and also one of the twelve.

3d. James the Just, son of Joseph, brother of our Lord, an Apostle added after the twelve, placed by the other Apostles in the Episcopal seat at Jerusalem, and aided by the Apostles, governed the Church, was president of the Apostolic Council, and being martyred, was succeeded in his Episcopate at Jerusalem by his cousin Simeon, the son of Cleophas.

If this treatise were designed to be purely historical and relating to *one* man, it might end here; but inasmuch as I was led to state in what light Mary was to be regarded, having proved her to have been both a wife and mother, so now, having shown the position which James held in the Church and connected him intimately with his successor, I will examine, by the light we have gained, that ministry which began with James and was transmitted to his successor. What was that to which it is said that Simeon succeeded by the unanimous appointment of the surviving Apostles, Disciples, and kinsmen of our Lord, who had known him in the flesh?

It would not be necessary to speak of the powers exercised by those called in Scripture and history *Apostles*, except to point out the difference betwixt them and their successors who are not called Apostles.

To say there never were but twelve Apostles—that the Apostolic office was not extended and continued, at least for a time—is to contradict the plainest Scripture and history. Again, to say there was no difference between the Apostles who founded the Churches and those who succeeded them in the government of them, is to confound things sufficiently unlike, at least, to be called in ancient history by different names.

Eusebius says, "There were many besides the twelve who were called Apostles" (B. I. 12). So we have found it.

When the Saviour ascended, He left the Church with but "*eleven*."

Matthias was added another Apostle (Acts, i. 26);
Barnabas was added another (Acts, xiv. 14);
Paul was added another;
James was added another (Gal. i. 19);
Silvanus was added another (1 Thes. i. 1, and ii. 6);
Timotheus was added another (1 Thes. i. 1, and ii. 6).

If these, or any of these were Apostles, then was not the Apostolic office limited to the twelve whilst they lived, neither did it die when they died.

If it should be said that Matthias was chosen in the place of Judas, it was done by the other Apostles after the ascension, and therefore it was a succession.

If it should be alleged that Paul was appointed in the place of some one else, unknown to us, and James in the place of some one else, unknown, and Barnabas in the place of some one else, and so on, that would be, so far, an Apostolic succession, a continuation of the Apostolic office.

If James, who came into the Apostleship after the twelve, was preferred before them, and Paul, who came in later, was "not a whit behind the very chiefest Apostles," then the rank held by those who came in later was not necessarily inferior to that held by the first, because they were later.

From the language employed by Eusebius in describing the solemn, public introduction of Simeon into the office vacated by James, it would seem, at first, as if that Episcopate, which lost nothing in passing from the twelve to James, lost nothing in passing from James to Simeon. The narrative continues on as naturally as the history of one king's succeeding to the throne vacated by another king.

This uninterrupted continuation of office, passing from the twelve to James and from James to Simeon, did not end with Simeon. Observe how unvaried and unbroken is the line of succession.

Says Eusebius (B. IV. 5): "So much have I learned from writers, that down to the invasion of the Jews under Adrian there were fifteen successions of Bishops in the Church at Jerusalem. * * In the mean time the Jews being subdued in the rebellion, as the Bishops from the circumcision failed, it may be necessary to recount them now in order from the first.

"The first, therefore, was James, the brother of our

Lord; after him, the second was Simeon, the third Justus, the fourth Zaccheus, the fifth Tobias, the sixth Benjamin, the seventh John, the eighth Matthias, the ninth Philip, the tenth Seneca, the eleventh Justus, the twelfth Levi, the thirteenth Epaphras, the fourteenth Joseph, the fifteenth and last Judas. And thus many were the Bishops of Jerusalem from the Apostles to the time we are treating of." He afterwards names all the Bishops from the Gentiles down to his own time, A. D. 325.

If we had no information on this subject but what is contained here, we could not help believing that the same office which was held by one of these men was held by all in succession.

We know what the first was: he was the Apostle James, of illustrious memory. We know who the second was, and with what solemnity he was introduced into the Episcopal seat at Jerusalem as the one "worthy to succeed James." Each of these was apparently the only Bishop in Jerusalem.

When shall we say that this Episcopal office, thus begun and thus continued, died out by natural limitation? Who was the last in the succession from the Apostles, and who was the first of a new order?

If the Apostleship was limited to the original twelve and a different ministry followed immediately after, which was the first Presbyterian, or Congregational, or Quaker minister? Was it the Apostle James, the Lord's brother? He was not one of the twelve. Was he only a Congregational or Quaker minister acting as Bishop over the "many thousands of believers," and presiding in council over Peter, and Paul, and

Barnabas, "Apostles, Elders, and Brethren?" Or was it under Simeon, or Justus, or Zaccheus, or Tobias that the Church became Presbyterian?

If Episcopacy came in after Apostolic days, which, in all this line of successions, was the first Episcopal Bishop, succeeding to what had been Presbyterian or Congregational?

Whilst we trace the unbroken chain of office, link by link, from an Apostle down, we notice that no one is here called an Apostle except James; and when placed at the head of this list, he is not called the first Apostle, but the first Bishop of Jerusalem. He is the only link fastened to the Rock above; the other links depend on him. Yet every link is in its place—the chain is entire.

What reason can we discover why the historians uniformly change the language from Apostle to Bishop, when speaking of those who succeeded to the same office? Why was James called an Apostle—but Simeon and Justus, not Apostles but Bishops?

Theodoret says that "those now called Bishops were anciently called Apostles; but in process of time the name of Apostle was left to those who were truly Apostles, and the name of Bishop was restrained to those who were anciently called Apostles." This is the assertion of a fact; but what are the reasons for the fact.

The word Apostle means one who is sent—a missionary: "As my Father hath sent me, even so send I you." The word Bishop means overseer. "Take heed to all the flock over which (ἐν ᾧ, in which) the Holy Ghost hath made you overseers"—Bishops (Acts, xx.

28). The first who were sent out by Christ to establish churches were literally Apostles—missionaries. Those who always continued in missionary work were never called any thing else but Apostles; such were Paul, Peter, Barnabas, and John. Those who became stationary and took the oversight of particular churches were called the Bishops of those churches. Such was James, who is called the first Bishop of Jerusalem: such was Timothy who is called the first Bishop of Ephesus. Eusebius says (Book III. 4), "Timothy is recorded as having first received the Episcopate at Ephesus, as Titus also was appointed over the churches in Crete."

Though Paul was an Apostle to the Ephesians and established the churches there, he is not called the first Bishop there, because he was not the resident overseer. Timothy, who before itinerated with Paul, organizing churches as an Apostle, and is called by Paul an Apostle (1 Thes. i. 1, and ii. 6), when he became established permanently over the churches of Ephesus, was ever after called the Bishop of Ephesus. The Elders (Presbyters) who had been called Bishops by Paul, because they were overseers in their respective congregations, were never called Bishops after Timothy became Apostolic Bishop over them. Calling Timothy the first Bishop of Ephesus does not conflict with the claims of Paul the founder, nor with the claims of the Elders. Their oversight *in* their congregations was different from his, for Timothy had the oversight of them all.

James and Timothy were called Apostles, as they stood in one relation to the Church, and Bishops, as they stood in another relation. Apostle refers to their commission as sent to the churches, and Bishop refers to their duties as overseers to their flocks.

The same is true of St. Mark as of James and Timothy. Eusebius (B. II. 16): "Mark, they say, being the first that was sent to Egypt, proclaimed the Gospel there which he had written, and first established churches in the city of Alexandria." (B. II. 24):* "In the eighth year of the reign of Nero, Anianus succeeded the Apostle and Evangelist Mark in the government of the churches at Alexandria."

Mark, who began as deacon, and then became Evangelist, afterwards was sent to Egypt as an Apostle to found the churches; then as Bishop he resided there and governed them. Anianus did not succeed Mark as an Evangelist to write a Gospel; not as Apostle to found the churches, but as Bishop to govern them.

The churches of Jerusalem, Ephesus, and Alexandria were privileged to have an Apostle for their first Bishop. Some eminent churches, such as Rome, had not. Paul first preached the Gospel in Rome, as we read in Acts, yet is he not called the first Bishop of Rome; for though he had "the care of all the churches," still he never, as resident Bishop, had the oversight of any.

Eusebius writes (B. III. 1): "Peter appears to have preached through Pontus, Galatia, Bithynia, Cappadocia, and Asia, to the Jews that were scattered abroad; who also, finally, coming to Rome, was crucified with

* These quotations are made from Crusé's translation, following the Regius edition, which has the correct text in this place. "Athanasius in his Synopsis calls both Mark and Luke Apostles."—VALESIUS.

his head downwards." (Ch. ii.): "After the martyrdom of Paul and Peter, Linus was the first that received the Episcopate at Rome." Though Paul founded the Church at Rome, and Peter, "finally," in his travels among the dispersed Jews in Asia, came there, neither of these Apostles is ever called Bishop of Rome, for neither resided there, as James resided at Jerusalem. Linus was the first Bishop of Rome, as Timothy was the first Bishop of Ephesus, and James the first Bishop of Jerusalem.*

It is observable that the Scriptures maintain the same guarded silence about Peter's ever being at Rome, that they do respecting the last days of Mary, and doubtless for the same wise reason, that those who make a goddess of the one and a demigod of the other, should not be able to glean from inspiration so much as one grain of sand for a foundation to build upon.

It is true, Peter himself does date one of his Epistles from "Babylon" (1 Pet. v. 13), and from the exact cor-

---

* In numbering the Roman Bishops, Eusebius always begins with Linus, and counts from the Apostles in this way. (B. V. 6): The blessed Apostles, having founded and established the Church, transmitted the office to Linus. (B. III. 2): "After the martyrdom of Paul and Peter, Linus was the first that received the Episcopate at Rome." (III. 4): "Linus has been before shown to be the first after Peter that received the Episcopate at Rome." (V. 6): Linus was succeeded by Anancletus, and after him Clement held the Episcopate the third from the Apostles." (IV. 1): Alexander, the fifth in succession from Peter and Paul."

Though Paul and Peter are thus referred to as having laid the foundation of the Church at Rome, the list of Roman Bishops is never headed with the name of Paul or Peter, though Paul first and often labored there, and Peter went there to preach and die. The catalogue of the Jerusalem Bishops begins distinctly with "first James, second Simon, third Justus."

respondence between the history of the Church of Rome and the description of Babylon, in the seventeenth chapter of Revelations, there can be no doubt but that Peter by *Babylon* meant Rome, and that his prophetic eye saw what John saw, and what after ages have seen in that "Babylon, that Mystery of iniquity."

Eusebius (B. II. 15) says: "Peter makes mention of Mark in the first epistle, which he is said to have composed in the city of Rome, and that he shows this fact by calling the city by an unusual trope, 'Babylon'" 1 Pet. v. 13). As Eusebius was not a prophet, like Peter, he did not see how exactly the Church of Rome in later times, when the papacy should be established and supremacy asserted, would correspond with John's description. Rome, in the time of Eusebius, had not become what it has been since, or Eusebius would have understood why Peter did not connect his name with Rome, and why, like St. John, he called her Babylon.

Peter's labors as an Apostle amongst the dispersed Jews through Pontus, Galatia, Bithynia, Cappadocia, and Asia, stand out boldly in the Scriptures (1 Pet. i. 1); but that this obscure allusion to Babylon should be the only inspired intimation that he ever was at Rome, is something for a Roman rather to be ashamed of than to glory in.

Those Apostles, then, who never were restricted to a particular charge in the government of churches, were not called by any other title than Apostle; whilst those Apostles and their successors in office, who had the oversight of particular churches, were called in history the Bishops of those churches.

Again: there is another reason for calling some Apostles and others not.

Most of those whom we call Apostles enjoyed a privilege which their successors did not—they received their commission or instructions, or both, from the Lord Himself. Because it was known that Paul was not amongst the first and had not been ordained by an Apostle, his claim was questioned, and he was constrained to show "the proof of his Apostleship," that it was derived, not like that of some others by ordination, but from the original source by direct revelation. Thus does he speak of it (Gal. i. 1): "Paul an Apostle, not of men neither by man, but by Jesus Christ and God the Father." (Ver. 11): "I certify you, brethren, that the Gospel which was preached of me is not after man; for I neither received it of man, neither was I taught it, but by the revelation of Jesus Christ." "Am I not an Apostle? Am I not free? Have I not seen the Lord Jesus Christ? Are not ye my work in the Lord?" (1 Cor. ix. 1.)

That Paul saw the Lord in the way going to Damascus, explained how he could have been made an Apostle, though he had not been made so by man, as Matthias was in part. The mere fact of seeing the Lord Jesus Christ did not make Paul an Apostle, for He was seen of above five hundred brethren at once: but are all Apostles?

Again: to become an Apostle it was not necessary to obtain it directly from the Lord. Timothy, a young man found by Paul in Lystra (Acts, xvi. 1), the son of a Greek, doubtless never saw the Lord; yet he is declared by St. Paul to be entitled to the prerogatives of an Apostle (1 Thes. i. 1, and ii. 6). He received both commission and instructions from St. Paul. (2 Tim. i. 6): "Stir up the gift of God which is on thee by the putting on of my hands." (2 Tim. ii. 2): "The things that thou hast heard of me among many witnesses, the same commit thou to faithful men, who shall be able to teach others also."

Though there were such exceptions, yet as a general rule those called Apostles enjoyed a nearer connection with Christ, which gave them an advantage above their successors.

As the distinction, however, between an Apostle and a Bishop was not technical, not a distinction of office, for the same man was called both, it would be difficult to draw the line and say definitely who was entitled to be called an Apostle and who not, but only Bishop.

Again: there was another advantage which the Apostles, in common with others in the Apostolic age, enjoyed above their successors, their ability to confirm their words by signs and wonders and divers miracles, gifts of the Holy Ghost, the gift of tongues, and healing, and prophecy. Though these gifts and graces did not belong exclusively to the Apostles, their successors, at least to any great extent, did not have them. These things certainly gave great pre-eminence to those early Fathers in the Church who possessed them. Still, these things did not pertain to any office, high or low. They were personal to each man, and did not make him to be an Apostle who had them, nor exclude him from the office who had them not. The world, however, has attached importance to them, and agreed to honor the men who were distinguished by them.

Whether any or all of the reasons here assigned influenced the historians to call some in the same line of office Apostles and others Bishops, there were reasons satisfactory to themselves, and this is reason enough for us to leave the title of Apostle to those whom we find so called in history, and call the succession in the ministry an Episcopal succession—a succession to the Episcopate derived from the Apostles, rather than a succession to the Apostolate. We are content to leave the subject where the early historians left it. The pioneers and founders of the Church, who possessed peculiar advantages and privileges, gifts and graces, and whose connection with the Saviour was very near, they called by the title of Apostle; to their successors, who, without these marked distinctions, were empowered, so far as ordination could empower them, to discharge officially the same duties, they gave the title of Bishop.

In Scripture, the title of Apostle only is given to the highest in the ministry; historians began the practice of calling them Bishops. In the expression concerning Judas, "his bishopric let another take," there is an intimation that they were to become Bishops, but no one is so called. In Scripture, James the Lord's brother is called Apostle; historians call him the first Bishop of Jerusalem. Simeon is styled the second Bishop of Jerusalem. Whether the distinction between an Apostle and a Bishop be more or less, we may say, without doing violence to truth or history, Simeon succeeded to the Episcopate, but not to the Apostolate of James.

The theory of an Apostolic ministry is, that it is derived from Christ, through those whom he empowered to organize and govern the Church. Civil power may be conferred by the governed on their rulers; but the Christian ministry comes from Christ down to the people. The laity did not ordain the Deacons, then the Deacons the Elders, and the Elders the Bishops or Apostles. It was by the putting on of the Apostles' hands the first ordination was conferred. When one was admitted in this way to be a Deacon or Elder or Bishop, he received a part of the Apostolic ministry. Those Elders whom Titus ordained in every city of Crete, obtained part of the same ministry which Titus had, but not the whole—not that part of it which would authorize them to ordain others. If one of these Elders had taken upon him to ordain, without having received authority to do so, a ministry thus begun would not have been Apostolic.

To give a man jurisdiction over a diocese or parish, is different from ordaining him. Jurisdiction may be variously conferred. "Peter, James, and John, with perhaps others, promoted James to be Bishop of Jerusalem (Eus., B. II. 1). The surviving Apostles, disciples, and kinsmen of our Saviour appointed Simeon to succeed James (Eus., B. III. 11). Paul sent Titus to Crete to set in order and ordain. In England the crown nominates a man to be Bishop of a particular diocese, the Dean and Chapter of that diocese confirm; but all this does not make him Bishop, it only confers on him legal jurisdiction: his ordination must be by Bishops' hands. In the Protestant Episcopal Church in the United States, the clergy, in convention assembled, nominate, the laity concur, the majority of the standing committees and of the Bishops of the several Dioceses in the Union confirm; this confers jurisdiction. The putting on of a Bishop's hands, assisted always by two or more Bishops, confers on him authority to exercise the office of a Bishop in the Church of Christ.

Nearly in the same sense that the King is head of the Church in England, the Clergy in Convention are head in the United States. They take the initiative and *nominate*, but in neither case do they ordain. Ordination by the people, or a Deacon, or an Elder, would be a departure from an Apostolic ministry, because the power to ordain is not conferred on a layman, Deacon, or Elder, but is always expressly reserved to the Bishop. Every Deacon and Presbyter knows that he receives authority to exercise his office; but not to confer it on others. A man though lawfully married, is not thereby authorized to marry others. A lieutenant or captain in the army has his own duties, but to issue commissions to make others lieutenants or captains like himself is not one of his duties.

If there was a sufficient distinction between an Apostle and a Bishop to call them by different names, and yet there was an unbroken succession of Bishops from the Apostles, the question arises, what was transmitted from the first to the second, and from the second to the third? It is safe to say, just that legal authority which could be conferred by ordination, and which would be necessary to perpetuate the same Church in all its integrity. This would not include the gift of tongues, the power of working miracles, nor any of those peculiar and personal advantages which the founders of Christianity enjoyed; but which were not necessary in after times, neither to sustain the Church as it was received from the Apostles, nor to perpetuate it as received to those who should come after always, even to the end of the world.

Authority to do what St. Paul, in his Epistles, instructs Timothy to do at Ephesus and Titus in Crete, could be conveyed perpetually by ordination. Such authority committed to faithful men would sustain and leave the Church of Christ, at the end of time, the same Church that it was at the beginning. Authority to do these things, disconnected from inspired guidance and supernatural gifts, is all that is claimed by those who, through a regular succession of ordinations from the Apostles, now exercise the office of Bishop in the Church of Christ.

Great pains have ever been taken to perpetuate such a ministry in every ancient Church.

Not only at Jerusalem was the succession in the Episcopate preserved, but Eusebius continues the catalogues of Bishops in succession from the Apostles, by name, number, and date in several of the Churches, down to his own time. Nor did the succession stop there because Eusebius died. Where the Churches have retained their organizations, as many have, their successions of Bishops are preserved to the present day.

We cannot find a time, from the Apostles down, when there were not thus Bishops in the Churches. We have seen that they were in the beginning; we find them in the Church now, and we find them at every intervening period from the beginning till now.

The original constitution and ministry of the Church was *Episcopal*, as distinguished from *Papacy* on the one hand and *Parity* on the other. There never was a time when there were not Episcopal Churches, and for many centuries we find no mention or trace of any other. For several ages there was no Papacy. There is not the remotest allusion to it in Scripture nor in the early historians. Certainly there was no exhibition of Papacy or supremacy in Peter; we find none of it at Rome.

Since no claim to supremacy is made by the mother Church at Jerusalem, nor to the Papacy by a successor of James the Lord's brother, once the presiding Bishop, no claim to supremacy or Papacy from any other source can be sustained by facts, or be defended by argument and reason.

Some *hold to* an Apostolic ministry so exclusively, that they consider those acting in a ministry not thus derived as guilty of sin.

Some are *attached* to it from *principle*, believing it a duty to receive and perpetuate the Church and ministry which were established at first.

Some *adhere* to it from *expediency*, to avoid schisms or divisions and distractions.

Some are *satisfied* that they are acting under an Apostolic commission, but if their ordination had been less regular they would not regard it of sufficient importance to seek a better.

Some *happen* to be in an Apostolic Episcopal ministry, but could not give an answer to any man who should ask them a reason why they came in, nor wherefore such a ministry should be preferred.

With all these differences of *opinion*, men may *act* harmoniously in the same Church.

Others there are whose ordination to the ministry

was not thus regularly and Apostolically derived, who now wish with more or less earnestness that they had examined this subject earlier in life.

The Ordinal in the Prayer-Book of the Protestant Episcopal Church in the United States, says: "It is evident unto all men diligently reading Holy Scripture and ancient authors, that from the Apostles' times there have been these orders of ministers in Christ's Church—Bishops, Priests, and Deacons."*

Here the Protestant Episcopal Church, without determining the value of such an Apostolic Episcopal ministry, asserts a well-known fact, and then acts as if it were, to say the least, worthy to be regarded, by requiring all who minister to her congregations to obtain their ordination from this primitive source, by the putting on of the hands of an Apostolic Bishop.

> "Full blest are they, and only they,
> Who from God's judgments never stray;
> Who know what's right, not only so,
> But always practice what they know."

How can we be assured that the connection in the Episcopal ordinations has been uninterrupted, so that we have the same ministry now which began with the Apostles and was transmitted from them?

How this ministry began, and how carefully its successions were preserved and recorded, every name in its place, has here been shown from Eusebius, for the first three hundred and twenty-five years.

---

* In Greek, "Presbyter;" then Prester, Priest. English, "Elder."

Tracing from our own times back, every Bishop's consecration in the Protestant Episcopal Church in the United States, and in the Church of England throughout her dominions, is definitely known. For three hundred and fifty years back the name of every Bishop, the date of his consecration, and the names of his consecrators, are known. I have them before me as I write.*

To avoid mistakes or imposture, three Bishops at least are always required to lay on hands in every Episcopal consecration. Sometimes there were as many as six; they average above four.

As an illustration of the extreme care with which these consecrations are guarded from accident or wrong, take this example. Charles Pettit McIlvaine was consecrated to be Bishop of Ohio, October 31st, 1832, by Bishops William White, Alexander V. Griswold, and William Meade, three Bishops. (If one only of these three had been a lawful Bishop, it would have been a consecration; but for security three officiated.) These three, White, Griswold, and Meade, were consecrated by fourteen others, each of whose names we know and have the records; and those four teen by fifty-two others, each of whose names we know.

In this geometrical ratio are the safeguards of Episcopal consecrations multiplied. If any precaution can make assurance doubly sure, then the validity of the consecration of our Bishops is secured beyond a doubt.

---

* Perceval gives the volume and page for each, in the original records.

If tracing back the ecclesiastical genealogy of one Bishop, involves in the first generation the participation of three Bishops, in the second, fourteen, and in the third generation fifty-two Bishops, the line of descent is not by a single thread. The probability is, that every living Bishop in Europe or America, whose ordination has been regular for ages past, has had a thread leading back through different lines to every Apostle who ordained in Europe, Western Asia, or Africa. I could sooner believe this, than that the Apostolical ordination had at any time ceased, and a new order of Bishops throughout the world, nobody knows when, had taken their place.

As every man has two parents, four grandparents, and eight great-grandparents, tracing back a few generations, instead of proving that he is related to nobody, may show that he is allied to a multitude of families, and an inheritance may descend to him through any one of them.

As the consecrations of Bishops have ever been conducted with care and been matters of faithful record, they can be traced uninterruptedly back in the past as far as historical and legal records of any kind have escaped the wasting tooth of time. In proof of this I will here give the Episcopal genealogy of *one* Bishop in one line only, tracing the line as far back as three-hundred and fifty years, stating the name of the Bishop, when he was consecrated, for what Diocese and by what Bishops he was consecrated. What I here do for one Bishop, I could as readily do for any other in the Church of England and in the Protestant Episcopal Church in America.

BISHOPS.	BY WHOM CONSECRATED.
Charles Pettit McIlvaine, Oct. 31, 1832, Bp. of Ohio.	Wm. White, Bp. Pennsylvania. Alex. V. Griswold, Bp. Eastern Diocese. Wm. Meade, Bp. Virginia.
William White, Feb. 4. 1787, Bp. Pennsylvania.	John Moore, Abp. Canterbury, Eng. Wm. Markham, Abp. York. Charles Moss, Bp. Bath and Wells. John Hinchcliff, Bp. Peterboro.
John Moore, Bp. Bangor, Feb. 12, 1775; translated to Canterbury, 1782.	Frederic Cornwallis, Abp. Canterbury. Edmund Keene, Bp. Ely. Robert Lowth, Bp. Oxford. John Thomas, Bp. Rochester.
Frederic Cornwallis, Bp. Litchfield, Feb. 18, 1749; translated to Canterbury, 1768.	Thomas Herring, Abp. Canterbury. Joseph Wilcocks, Bp. Rochester. Martin Benson, Bp. Gloucester. Samuel Lisle, Bp. Norwich.
Thomas Herring, Bp. Bangor, Jan. 15, 1737; translated to Canterbury, 1747.	John Potter, Abp. Canterbury. Joseph Wilcocks, Bp. Rochester. Nicholas Claggett, Bp. St. David's. Thomas Secker, Bp. Oxford.
John Potter, Bp. Oxford, May 15, 1715; translated to Canterbury, 1737.	Jonathan Trelawny, Bp. Winchester. John Evans, Bp. Bangor. Wm. Wake, Bp. Lincoln. Richard Willis, Bp. Gloucester.
Jonathan Trelawny, Bp. Bristol, Nov. 8, 1685; translated to Winchester, 1707.	Wm. Sancroft, Abp. Canterbury. John Dolben, Abp. York. Henry Compton, Bp. London. Nath'l Crewe, Bp. Durham. Peter Mawes, Bp. Winchester. Thomas Lamplugh, Bp. Exeter. Francis Turner, Bp. Ely. Thomas Spratt, Bp. Rochester.
William Sancroft, Abp. Canterbury, Jan. 27, 1677.	Henry Compton, Bp. London. Seth Ward, Bp. Salisbury. John Dolben, Bp. Rochester. Joseph Henshaw, Bp. Peterboro. Peter Gunning, Bp. Ely. Thomas Lamplugh, Bp. Exeter.
Henry Compton, Bp. Oxford, Dec. 26, 1674; translated to London, 1675.	Gilbert Sheldon, Abp. Canterbury. George Morley, Bp. Winchester. Seth Ward, Bp. Salisbury. John Dolben, Bp. Rochester. Joseph Henshaw, Bp. Peterboro. Peter Gunning, Bp. Chichester.
Gilbert Sheldon, Bp. London, Oct. 18, 1660; translated to Canterbury, 1663.	Matthew Wren, Bp. Ely. Accepted Frewen, Abp. York. Bryan Duppa, Bp. Winchester. John Warner, Bp. Rochester. Henry King, Bp. Chichester.

BISHOPS.	BY WHOM CONSECRATED.
Matthew Wren, Bp. Hereford, Mar. 8, 1634; translated to Ely, 1638.	Wm. Laud, Abp. Canterbury. Walter Curl, Bp. Winchester. Francis White, Bp. Ely. Joseph Hall, Bp. Exeter. Wm. Murray, Bp. Llandaff.
William Laud, Bp. St. David's, Nov. 18, 1621; translated to Canterbury, 1633.	George Monteigne, Bp. London. John Thornborough, Bp. Worcester. Nicholas Felton, Bp. Ely. George Carlton, Bp. Chichester. John Howson, Bp. Oxford.
George Monteigne, Bp. Lincoln, Dec. 14, 1617; translated to London, 1621.	George Abbott, Abp. Canterbury. Mark A. De Dominis, Abp. Spalatro. John King, Bp. London. Launcelot Andrews, Bp. Ely. John Buckeridge, Bp. Rochester. John Overall, Bp. Litchfield.
George Abbott, Bp. Litchfield, Dec. 3, 1609; translated to Canterbury, 1611.	Richard Bancroft, Abp. Canterbury. Launcelot Andrews, Bp. Ely. Richard Neyle, Bp. Rochester.
Richard Bancroft, Bp. London, May 3, 1597; translated to Canterbury, 1604.	John Whitgift, Abp. Canterbury. John Young, Bp. Rochester. Anthony Rudd, Bp. St. David's. Richard Vaughan, Bp. Bangor. Anthony Watson, Bp. Chichester.
John Whitgift, Bp. Worcester, April 21, 1577; translated to Canterbury, 1583.	Edmund Grindall, Abp. Canterbury. John Aylmer, Bb. London. Robt. Horne, Bp. Winchester. Richard Curteis, Bp. Chichester.
Edmund Grindall, Bp. London, Dec. 21, 1559; translated to Canterbury, 1573.	Matthew Parker, Abp. Canterbury. John Hodskin, Bp. Bedford. Wm. Barlow, Bp. Chichester. John Scory, Bp. Hereford.
Matthew Parker, Abp. Canterbury, Dec. 17, 1559.	John Hodskin, Bp. Bedford. Wm. Barlow, Bp. Chichester. John Scory, Bp. Hereford. Miles Coverdale, (late) Bp. Exeter.
John Hodskin, Bp. Bedford, Dec. 9, 1537.	Robert Parfew, Bp. St. Asaph. John Stokesley, Bp. London. John Hilsay, Bp. Rochester.
Robert Parfew, Bp. St. Asaph, July 2, 1536.	Thomas Cranmer, Abp. Canterbury. John Capon, Bp. Bangor. Wm. Rugg, Bp. Norwich.
Thomas Cranmer, Abp. Canterbury, Mar. 30, 1533.	John Longland, Bp. Lincoln. Henry Standish, Bp. St. Asaph. John Voysey, Bp. Exeter.
John Longland, Bp. Lincoln, May 5, 1521.	Wm. Warham, Abp. Canterbury. John Fisher, Bp. Rochester. Nicholas West, Bp. Ely. John Voysey, Bp. Exeter.

I have here traced the Episcopal genealogy of Bishop McIlvaine, of Ohio, back beyond the date when all non-episcopal organizations had their beginning. During this period of three hundred and fifty years, as we have every name and date from official records, there is hardly the possibility of an interruption; and the same precaution which has been observed during these years, so far as I know and believe, was observed throughout the entire line back to the Apostles. We have not all the official records, it is true, neither have we the original Gospels in the handwriting of the Evangelists; but we have multiplied copies.

If there were a landed proprietor whose title-deeds could be made out so clearly for 350 years, with the strongest presumptive proofs that they extended back 1800 years, and I should seek to dispossess him, not because I had ever been in possession, but on the ground that *possibly* in ages past before these 350 years, there may have been a break in his titles, though I know of none, such a plea would not be allowed in any court to invalidate an old title in him, nor to establish a new one in me. A cautious purchaser would say, the old is better.

With the same confidence that we believe that Christianity has been preserved in the world, and will be till it cover the whole earth, may we believe that an Apostolic ministry has been continued, and that one regularly consecrated a Bishop in the Protestant Episcopal Church in the United States has received part of this ministry, the same which he would have received if his consecration had been, like that of Timothy, by the hands of St. Paul himself.

Believing that the Protestant Episcopal Church has the two essential elements of a perfect Church—first, *holding the faith once delivered to the Saints;* secondly, *having a regular Apostolic ministry*—we believe without a doubt, that she is a true branch of the Church of Christ.

Whilst laboring in the ministry of a Church which has these two essential elements of a perfect Church—evangelical truth and Apostolical order—I need no charitable construction to be put upon the fullest employment of all the piety, learning, and zeal which I can devote to this work. I can go forward with no *fears* lest my success should be in opposition to Christ's cause and His Church; with no *faint hopes* that my ministry may be blessed, though not of His original ordaining; but with a firm confidence that all my efforts in this line are directed to the object which He would establish, and all I accomplish is so much done for His Church and for Him.

On the subject of adhering to that ministry which the Apostles established and perpetuated, Clement has this very pertinent paragraph in his Epistle to the Corinthians, section 44.*

"Our Apostles knew by our Lord Jesus Christ, that contentions should arise on account of the ministry, and therefore, having a perfect foreknowledge of this,

---

* Of Clement and this Epistle, Eusebius thus writes (B. III. 15, 16): "When Anancletus had been Bishop of Rome twelve years, he was succeeded by Clement, who the Apostle, in his Epistle to the Phillippians, shows had been his fellow-laborer, in these words—'with Clement and the rest of my fellow-laborers, whose names are in the book of life.' Of this Clement there is one Epistle extant, acknowledged as genuine, of considerable length and of great merit."

they appointed persons, as we before said, and then gave a direction in what manner, when they should die, other chosen and approved men should succeed in their ministry. Wherefore we cannot think that those may be justly thrown out of their ministry who were appointed by them, or afterwards chosen by other eminent men with the consent of the whole Church."

One *practical* result of acting on the principle that a pure faith only is essential to a Christian Church, and that any band of pious men may organize themselves into a new Church, as good as any that was before it, is this: that in some towns of considerable magnitude there are several houses for religious worship; but the people, not considering that adherence to an Apostolic ministry is of binding obligation, have divided and subdivided into new, and still newer denominations, till there are not left adherents enough to any one to have a Church or regular worship of any kind.

Bishop Smith, of Kentucky, relates that "when he expressed to a non-episcopal minister of Louisville his regrets at the ruinous subdivisions of Christians, he replied, that he had lately found in a rural district in Illinois, sixteen different denominations represented in seventeen families!"* If but half of this were true, what point does it give to St. Paul's expostulation with the Corinthians! (1 Cor. i. 10–15.) What is to become of these fractions of denominations?

---

* The Bishop of Kentucky assures the author that this statement is authentic.

If it be allowable in any age to draw together disciples and organize them into a new and separate Church, to work side by side with the acknowledged ministers of Christ, but not working with them, surely the Apostles individually might have done the same, and they did not want for opportunities. When the Corinthians were saying, "I am of Paul, and I of Apollos, and I of Cephas," if they had taken advantage of their personal popularity, and organized separate Churches, though they had kept so near the common faith that they had mutually sent and received corresponding members to their assemblies, it would have been as harmless a division of the one body of Christ as we can imagine. Yet even this the Apostles deprecated. They would make any sacrifice to avoid divisions. Paul, for this one reason, abstained from baptizing, lest any should say that he had baptized in his own name. If they could not always agree on questions of expediency, as Paul and Barnabas differed about taking Mark with them—though they parted company, they continued in the same ministry, and in the same Church. And Mark, who caused the contention, Paul afterwards sent for to assist him (2 Tim. iv. 11). And this Mark became an Evangelist and an Apostle (Eusebius, B. II. 16, 24), and established the Church in Alexandria; but his was part of that same Church and ministry from which no difference of opinion, no diversity of gifts or of popularity, could ever divide them.

If I really believed that the Church had become extinct on earth, and its ministry had expired, and I and my friends alone were left alive, I should have little hope that I could establish others more permanent and more successful. Where Christ and His Apostles had failed, what could I do? But they have not failed. There is diffused over the earth, and now in active life, at least one branch of the Church of Christ whose ministry has been derived unquestionably from the Apostles, and whose articles of faith embrace the truth as it is in Jesus.

I may ask myself the question, as I am often asked by others, what is my duty towards those who act in the name of Christ, and preach Him of *good-will*, though not following with us in the fellowship of the Apostles? So far as this is a practical question, Christ has answered it. (Luke, ix. 49): "John said, Master, we saw one casting out devils in Thy name, and we forbade him, because he followeth not with us. And Jesus said, Forbid him not, for he that is not against us is for us." This man was commended, not for refusing to follow Christ with the Apostles, but for doing that which would aid their cause. This man was not laboring to build up an independent Church, in opposition to the Apostles. Christ did not encourage the twelve to separate from each other, and follow after that man. "He is doing a good work in his way; but what is that to thee? Follow thou me." "Would God all the Lord's people were prophets" (Num. xi. 29).

There are many such good men whose hearts are full of Christ—their preaching is not of envy and strife, but of good-will. I honor them for their love to Him whom I love. So long as they sincerely labor to build on the only Foundation, Christ Jesus, I have not the heart to forbid them. That Christ is preached I therein rejoice. I have more sympathy with good men who follow not with the Apostles, than with Judas who was one of them. The respect which I entertain for them is for their personal worth, not for the sacredness of the organizations which they have made, and their successors may unmake.

But for that Church which was from the beginning, which is now steadfast in the Apostles' doctrine and fellowship, holding fast the form whilst contending earnestly for the faith, I feel more than a personal respect. The members individually in communion with such a Church I esteem according to their personal piety; but for the Church itself I have a reverence as an institution of Christ. Her ministry I regard as of divine appointment; her liturgy as preserving a pure faith, and promoting devotion; her doctrines those which "can be proved by most certain warrants of Holy Scripture." Though like Israel of old, she has passed through many vicissitudes in the Red Sea of persecution, in the wilderness of worldliness, at times has departed from the faith, and even been in bondage to Babylon, now I find her seated on her own loved Zion again, cured of her idolatry, and I rejoice to minister in her sanctuary.

This ministry I would employ to win men to the faith of Christ, that believing in Him they may have life through His name, and being justified by faith they may have peace with God. To preach the truth as it is in Jesus; to build up believers on their most holy faith; to minister to them the appointed means of grace, the Word and sacraments: these, as a Presbyter, are my duties. As an officer in the army of

God's sacramental host, I am expected to perform these services, but not to commission others. That all who profess and call themselves Christians may be led into the way of truth, and hold the faith in unity of spirit, in the bond of peace, and in righteousness of life, this is my prayer.

The vows which bind me to the Protestant Episcopal Church were made with my head, my heart, my tongue. I cannot and would not recall them. With no doubts or misgivings, I can labor in this Church, built on the foundation of the Apostles and Prophets, Jesus Christ Himself being the chief corner-stone.

"I prize her heavenly ways,
Her sweet communion, solemn vows,
Her hymns of love and praise.

"For her my tears shall fall,
For her my prayers ascend,
To her my cares and toils be given,
Till toils and care shall end."

COLLECT.

"O Almighty God, who hast built Thy Church on the foundation of the Apostles and Prophets, Jesus Christ Himself being the chief corner-stone, grant that, by the operation of the Holy Ghost, all Christians may be so joined together in unity of spirit and in the bond of peace, that they may be a holy temple acceptable unto Thee. Give them the abundance of Thy grace, that with one heart they may desire the prosperity of Thy holy Apostolic Church, and with one mouth may profess the faith once delivered to the Saints. Defend them from the sins of heresy and schism; let not the foot of pride come nigh to hurt them, nor the hand of the ungodly to cast them down. And grant that the course of this world may be so peaceably ordered by Thy governance, that Thy Church may joyfully serve Thee in all godly quietness; that so they may walk in the ways of truth and peace, and at last be numbered with Thy Saints in glory everlasting, through Thy merits, O blessed Jesus, Thou gracious Bishop and Shepherd of our souls, who art with the Father and the Holy Ghost one God, world without end. *Amen.*"

APPENDIX
TO
JAMES THE LORD'S BROTHER.

———o———

The argument in the first part of this treatise was intentionally condensed into the smallest space possible, to adapt it to popular use. The notice which has been taken of the work by the press, and the questions that have been asked, have shown the author what points in the discussion needed to be brought out more distinctly, and where additional light was required. I will therefore expand more fully the answer to the objection, "why, if Jesus had brothers, did He commit his Mother to the care of John?" Answering this question will give me an opportunity also to correct an error of those who differ from me, which was allowed to go on page 22 unnoticed, because all the reasonings and conclusions of my argument would be the same, even though that error were permitted to stand.

Those who deny that our Lord had a brother James, assume, what is not the fact, that the sons of Cleophas were cousins to Christ, *because their mother Mary was sister to his mother Mary.* This assumption, that those two Marys were sisters, is *essential* to their theory, but does not in any way affect mine. I proved that there was such a person as James the Lord's brother, even granting this assumption to be true, and giving it full force. I will now prove that it is not true; that the two Marys were not sisters, and therefore there is no foundation whatever for the argument of my opponents. The truth is, that Jesus and the children of Cleophas were cousins, because *Joseph* and *Cleophas* were *brothers*, and not because *Mary* and *Mary* were *sisters*.

I will presently show the exact relationship of all the parties mentioned in connection with this subject, and that will make the argument of this book still stronger and clearer.

It has been asserted that Jesus had no brothers; because on the cross He consigned his mother to the care of the disciple whom He loved.

This conclusion does not necessarily follow. Men, having both brothers and children, often appoint as executors of their wills, and guardians of their families, persons who are not related to them. There are some good reasons, which I will now give, why Christ should commit his mother to the protection of John. When all the other disciples forsook their Master and fled, John followed him into the palace of the High Priest, (John, xviii. 15,) and had followed, in company with the women, to the place of execution, and was standing there within sight and hearing of Jesus, and by the side of his mother. He was then in a situation to receive a dying request from the lips of Christ. So far his *position* was favorable.

John also was near of kin to Christ; he was own blood cousin to Him; because *John's mother* was *sister* to *Jesus' mother*. This will appear by what follows.

The persons present, when Jesus consigned his mother

to John are thus named and described by three evangelists. (John, xix. 25,) "Now there stood by the cross of Jesus, His mother, and his mothers' sister; Mary the wife of Cleophas, and Mary Magdalene." (Mark, xv. 40,) "There were also women looking on afar off, among whom was Mary Magdalene, and Mary the mother of James the Less and of Joses, and Salome." (Matt. xxvii. 56.) "And many women were there beholding afar off, among which was Mary Magdalene, and Mary the mother of James and Joses, and the mother of Zebedee's children."

These three accounts describe the same company; for Mary Magdalene is one of the persons in them all; and she could not have been in different places at the same time. It is one group differently described. In St. John the women are named by *pairs*, as the twelve apostles are by St. Matt. x. 2. thus :

"Simon, who is called Peter, and Andrew his brother ;
James the son of Zebedee, and John his brother;
Philip and Bartholomew ;
Thomas and Matthew the Publican ;
James the son of Alpheus, and Lebbeus, whose surname was Thaddeus ;
Simon the Canaanite, and Judas Iscariot."

This manner of placing the word "and," so as to class the persons named two and two, explains the language of St. John, who employs the same form of expression when telling us who were at the cross: "Now there stood by the cross of Jesus, His mother, and His mothers' sister ; Mary the wife of Cleophas, and Mary Magdalene. "This makes four persons, arranged in two pairs, in the same way that classifying the Apostles in six pairs, makes twelve.

How many of these women there were (whose names are given us) and who they were, will be made to appear distinctly by placing the accounts of the three evangelists side by side, so that we can compare the names and count them.

Now there stood by the cross of Jesus,

Mark xv. 40.	Matt. xxvii. 56.	John xix. 25.
1. Mary Magdalene,	1. Mary Magdalene.	1. Mary Magdalene.
2. Mary the mother of Jas. the Less, and Joses.	2. Mary the mother of James and Joses.	2. Mary the wife of Cleophas.
3. Salome,	3. Mother of Zebedee's children.	3. His mothers' sister.
		4. His mother.

Here are the same names as in the gospels, only so arranged in the last column that they can be compared with those in the two first. By this comparison it will be seen, that the woman who is described by John, as *Jesus's "mother's sister,"* is named by Mark, "*Salome,*" and called by Matthew, "*the mother* of *Zebedee's* children;" that is, *Salome, the mother of Zebedee's children,* was *Jesus's mother's* sister. As John was the son of Zebedee, Jesus and *John* were *cousins*; their *mothers* being sisters.

This perfectly agrees with the original Greek, as well as with the English translation, and is certainly more intelligible than the theory which makes *Mary*, the mother of Christ, and *Mary* the wife of Cleophas, to be sisters.

That cousins should have similar names, as the children of Joseph and Cleophas had, is not so strange; but that two sisters should have but *one* name *between them* is so unlikely, that we may be sure it is not the true meaning, especially since making Mary the wife of Cleophas to be sister to Jesus's mother, does violence to the plain language of scripture, besides striking out of the account entirely "*Salome*," "the mother of Zebedee's children." The reading which makes Salome, the mother of Zebedee's children, to be the sister of Mary, the mother of Jesus, brings in all the persons mentioned, makes good sense, is consistent both with the Greek and English, is according to the natural structure of the Scripture language, and makes the subject plain, intelligible and truth-like.

If St. John had meant us to understand that Mary the wife of Cleophas was sister to Mary the mother of Jesus, he knew how to write it, and he would have written it thus: "Now there stood by the cross of Jesus, his mother, and Mary his mother's sister, the wife of Cleophas, and Mary Magdalene." This is the way of writing names with epithets attached to them, thus: The Proverbs of Solomon the son of David, King of Israel. The name is put first, and not between the titles —it is not, The proverbs of the son of David, Solomon King of Israel.

Let us see what strange relationships we should establish among the Apostles by reading them as some read the names of those four women, so as to make but three out of four, and the two Marys, sisters:

1st, Simon, who is called Peter, and 2nd Andrew; 3rd, his brother James, the son of Zebedee; and 4th, John; 5th, his brother Philip; and 6th, Bartholomew; 7th, Thomas; and 8th, Matthew; 9th, the Publican James, the son of Alpheus.

Here, by false punctuation simply, two of the Apostles are separated from their real brothers, and allied to somebody else. Andrew is separated from Peter, and made brother to James the son of Zebedee; John is separated from his brother James, and made brother to Philip, in precisely the same way that some jumble together the names of the women at the cross, to make the two Marys sisters, reading them thus: "Now there stood by the cross of Jesus, 1st, his mother, and 2nd, His mother's sister, Mary the wife of Cleophas, and 3rd, Mary Magdalene. (This is identically the same kind of punctuation as above; 1st, Andrew; 2nd, his brother, James the son of Zebedee, and 3rd, John.) By this unnatural and false punctuation, *Salome*, Jesus's mother's sister, and mother of Zebedee's children, is *left out altogether*! So, instead of seeing by the cross of Christ, His mother, and Salome her sister, and Mary wife of Cleophas, and Mary Magdalene, we have only three Marys, *Mary* His mother, *Mary* her sister, and *Mary Magdalene*; but no Salome!

It is not St. John who is guilty of this confusion. He has used the appropriate language to describe four persons, in exactly the same way that St. Matthew has enumerated the twelve Apostles: Now there stood by the cross of Jesus, "His mother and his mother's sister;"—there are two; "Mary the wife of Cleophas and Mary Magdalene,"—there are four. These four women, as named and described by the three Evangelists in harmony, read thus: 1st, His Mother; and 2nd, Salome His mother's sister, the mother of Zebedee's children; 3rd, Mary the wife of Cleophas, mother of

James the Less and of Joses, and 4th, Mary Magdalene. Here I have only put into one sentence the three accounts in John, xix. 25, Mark, xv. 40, and Matt. xxvii. 56.

Salome the mother of John, being sister to the mother of Jesus, when He intrusted his mother to John, it was not only to a *beloved* disciple, a trustworthy man, who was on the spot; but to an own cousin, who had an interest in the family.

As John took his aunt to his own home, (John, xix 27,) it is certain *he* had a home to receive her. How long John was able to furnish a home to Mary his mother's sister, we do not know. That he did it for a time, does not prove that he did it because Jesus had not brothers. Though James the Lord's brother, was afterwards made Bishop of Jerusalem, it is possible that if he had been near to the cross at the time of the crucifixion, he may not then have been in a situation to give her a comfortable home. All homes are not equally desirable for such a purpose.

It seems to be proved that James had not children; possibly he may not have had a family into which to receive his mother. Judas a younger brother of our Lord, had children and "descendants, who continued to the days of the Emperor Trajan," (Eus. B. iii. 32) and they are spoken of in such a way as to imply that the older brothers had not descendants, (Eus. B. iii 19-20, (Cruse's translation.) "When the Emperor Domitian had issued his orders that the descendants of David should be slain, some of the heretics accused the descendants of *Judas*, as the *brother* of *our Savior*, according to the flesh; because they were of the family of David, and as such, were also related to Christ. * * There were yet living of the family of our Lord, the grandchildren of *Judas*, called the *brother of our Lord*, according to the flesh. These were reported as being of the family of David, and were brought to Domitian by Evocatus. For this Emperor was as much alarmed at the appearance of Christ as Herod. He put the question, if they were of David's race. They confessed that they were. He asked what property they had. Both of them answered, that they had between them, thirty-nine acres. They exhibited the hardness of their hands, caused by incessant labor. When he asked also respecting Christ and his kingdom; what was its nature, when and where it would appear; they replied, that it was not a temporal nor earthly Kingdom—that it would appear at the end of the world. Whereupon Domitian made no reply; but treating them with contempt as simpletons, commanded them to be dismissed."

Eusebius here speaks of *Judas* the *brother* of our Savior; as in the 32d chapter, he calls him, "one of the brothers of our Lord;" and brother in such a literal sense that his grand children were regarded as heirs to Jesus.

Those who deny that our Lord had brothers, or that His mother had sons, evade the force of the repeated declarations of both scripture and history, that He had brothers, by saying that "in *Hebrew*, *brother* sometimes means *cousin*." If brother did mean cousin in *Hebrew*, which it does not, literally speaking, that would not touch the case; for Eusebius did not write in *Hebrew*, but in Greek. The Gospels also were not written in

Hebrew, but in Greek. St. John, who speaks of Christ's brothers, (vii. 5.) did not write for Hebrews; for he explains to his readers the simplest Hebrew customs, telling them that the Passover was a feast of the Jews." (vi. 4.)

When the historian or the Evangelist meant *cousin*, he could say so, and say it in good Greek. Thus Eusebius, (B. iii. 11,) "Simeon the son of Cleophas, as they say, was (*anepsios*) cousin to our Savior; for Hegesippus relates that Cleophas was the *brother* of Joseph." Here is a word for cousin, *anapsios*, and also the word for brother, *adelphos*, in the same sentence. St. Luke represents Gabriel as saying to Mary, "Behold thy (*suggenes*) cousin Elizabeth, she hath also conceived," (Luke, I. 36.) St. Luke was not in want of a word for *cousin*; it is *suggenes*; and he uses it as often as he speaks of cousin or kinsman. (I. 58.) And her neighbors and her (*suggeneis*) cousins heard that the Lord had showed great mercy upon her." And again, (II. 44.) "They sought Him among their (*suggenesi*) kinsfolk and acquaintances." Again, (xiv. 12.) "When thou makest a dinner or a supper, call not thy friends nor thy (*adelphous*) brethren, nor thy (*suggeneis*) kinsmen." Here the proper words for *brothers* and for *kinsmen* occur in the same sentence. The Evangelists could express themselves in Greek, and say either *brother* or *cousin*, whichever they meant. So again, (Luke, xxi. 16.) "Ye shall be betrayed by parents (*adelphon*) brethren, and (*suggenon*) kinsfolk."

Many other places there are where the word *suggenes*, the proper word for cousin or kinsman, occurs in the N. Testament; as John, xviii. 26. L. I. 61. Acts, vii. 3, 14.

When we read of James the son of Zebedee, and John his *brother*; Simon Peter, and Andrew his *brother*, and Judas the *brother* of James, and James the Lord's *brother*, and Jesus the *brother* of James; as it is the same form of expression in every case, we should naturally understand that these persons were *brothers*, and not *cousins*, to each other. If the word brother means brother in one place, and cousin in another, by what rule of grammar, rhetoric, or logic, are we to distinguish them? We have the similar expressions:

"Jesus, the brother of James," (Mark. vi. 3,) and
"Jude, the brother of James," (Jude, i. 1.)

If brother means cousin, in one of these places, does it not in both? If it means cousin in only one, which is it?

When the Evangelists and historian were speaking of the cousins of our Lord, they used the proper words, *anepsios*, or *suggenes*; so when they are speaking of a brother, they say *adelphos*, which, denoting a particular relationship, never means *cousin*, but always *brother*.

When the Jews reproached Christ with being of a mean family, because He was the Carpenter's son, and *brother* to James and Joses and Simon and Judas, and his sisters were all in the neighborhood, there would have been no force in these taunting words, if He had had neither brother nor sisters, only distant relatives. When the Evangelists are speaking of the sisters of Jesus, (Matt, xiii. 56, and Mark, vi. 3,) they say *adelphai*, which meaning a *particulnr* relationship, as it does here, never means *cousins*; but alway *sisters*.

In complimentary speech it is allowable to give flattering titles, to be understood as figures of rhetoric; as David said, "I am distressed for thee, my brother Jonathan," (2. Sam. I. 26.) But in every instance in which the brothers and sisters of our Lord are mentioned, the Evangelist or historian is narrating *plain history*, in *plain prose*, meaning not only those who were "of his own kin; but in his own house." And since it is proved that they could say cousin, if they desired it; when they have told us distinctly and repeatedly that Christ had brothers, as well as cousins, it is evident that they meant just what they said; when they wrote *brothers*, it was brothers that they meant.

If the brothers and sisters of Jesus had been only cousins, the word for *cousin* would have been somewhere used; but it is not. The words, *father*, *mother*, *uncle*, *aunt*, *brother*, *sister*, in plain historical writing, are to be understood literally, unless there is something in the narrative to show that they are figurative, and cannot be literal. According to this well known rule, our Lord had both brothers and sisters, in the same sense that He had a mother; and His mother had both sons and daughters, as well as a husband. "Then Joseph her husband, being a just man, (Matt. I, 19.) did as the angel of the Lord had bidden him, and took unto him his wife," (24), "Is not this the carpenter's son? and is not his mother called Mary? and his brethren James and Joses and Simon and Judas? And his sisters, are they not all with us?" Matt., xiii, 55.)

We are told that the Emperor Domitian feared the grandchildren of Judas the brother of our Savior, as dangerous rivals for the throne of Judea, (Euseb. B. iii. 19.) They would have been legal heirs to David, through Joseph and Jesus, provided there had been no descendants of an older brother. That Domitian seized on the grandchildren of Judas, as next heirs to the King of the Jews, seems to imply, that there were no children of James to stand before them.

Though the fact that the descendants of Judas were the oldest representatives of the family of Jesus, would not, taken by itself, go to the extent of proving that James, an older brother, had not on the day of the crucifixion, a a family and a home most suitable for accommodating his mother; yet, taken in connexion with the fact that *John had* such a *home*, and, whilst the brethren of Jesus did not for some time believe in Him, John was from the beginning a devoted disciple; was one of the three on the Mount of transfiguration, (Matt. xvii. 1;) was one of the three in the Garden of Gethsemane; was a fast friend, not frightened as others were, by the sight of soldiers or the cross; was also near of kin to Jesus; and was in company with Mary, where both could be addressed from the cross, removes all ground of surprise that our Lord, though having brothers, committed his mother to the filial care of his cousin, "the disciple whom He loved."

This transaction, and the other subjects introduced into this discussion, will be better understood by having at one view before the eye, the exact relationship which all the parties named bear to Christ and to each other, showing every person's relation to every other person; I therefore here invite the attention of the reader to a close and critical investigation of the following table of

THE GENEALOGY

of our Lord, according to the flesh, for thirty generations, on the side of Joseph (through whom, according to the law, He was heir to the throne of David,) and for forty-three generations on the side of Mary, his mother. The genealogy through Joseph is found in Matt. I. from verse 6—that through Mary in Luke, III. from verse 23. The connection of Cleophas with the house of David is found in Eus., B. iii, 11, & II, 1. The Grand-children of "Judas, the brother of our Savior," Eusebius, B. iii, p. 20. The brothers and sisters of Jesus, Matt. xiii. 55.

Those in the royal line of heirship are in capitals; those descended from David, but not in the line of succession, are in Italics; these connected by marriage are in Roman Letters.

For Salome compare Mark, xv. 40,
" " " Matt. xxvii. 56,
" " " John, xix. 25.

(Matthew, I. 6.) 1. DAVID. (Luke, III. 23.)

2. SOLOMON.	2. *Nathan.*
3. REHOBOAM.	3. *Mattatha.*
See Matt. I. 7 to 15.	See Luke, III. 24 to 31.
26. JACOB.	41. *Heli.*
27. JOSEPH and CLEOPHAS.	42. *Mary* and *Salome.*

The last four were married thus :

27. JOSEPH. 42. MARY..	Zebedee. 42. *Salome.*	27. CLEOPHAS, Mary.
28 JESUS and JAMES THE JUST. and JOSES and SIMON and JUDAS, and their sisters. 40. GRANDSONS of JUDAS brother of our Savior.	43. *James the Great,* and *John.*	28. JAMES THE LESS, and JOSES and JUDAS and SIMEON.

The three Jameses are here seen in their proper relations to our Lord and to each other.

1, James the Just, son of Joseph and Mary, and brother of Jesus,

2, James the Great, son of Zebedee and Salome, brother of John.

3, James the Less, son of Cleophas and Mary, brother of Judas.

That Jesus did on the cross consign his mother to John, though heretofore we found her always in company with those called "*His brethren*", is a fixed fact. If I have not assigned sufficient reasons for it, proving John to have been own cousin to our Lord, how will those explain it who make John no relation to Jesus, and say that Christ had brothers only in the sons of Cleophas?

Let them show more clearly than I have done, the relationship of all these parties and vindicate Christ more satisfactorily from the charge of "preferring a mere neighbor to a brother, and doing what is repugnant to all the instincts of humanity."

Now contrast with the full exhibition given above, of all the facts and persons connected with this subject, that other theory which strikes out of existence James the Just, son of Joseph and Mary, the Lord's brother—omits all mention of Salome the mother of Zebedee's children—takes no notice of the relationship between Joseph and Cleophas—makes Mary wife of Cleophas, sister to Mary wife of Joseph—calls James the Less, son of Cleophas, "the Lord's brother," and denies that our Lord had a brother.

Here is the genealogy according to that false theory :

1. David.

2. SOLOMON.	2. *Nathan.*
27. JOSEPH.	42. *Mary* and *Mary*, Cleophas.
28. JESUS.	43. *James* the Less and *Judas*.
	45. *Grandsons* of Judas, the brother of our Savior.

This table cannot be correct; because it makes the "gandsons of "Judas the *brother* of our Savior," to be the descendants of another Judas who was not the Lord's brother, and not only so, but it makes the Judas whose grandsons Domitian feared, as heirs to the royal house of David, not to be of the royal line of David, nor heirs, at all ; for Mary the mother of Jesus, was 42 generations removed from David, and even at that, she was a descendant, not of Solomon and the line of kings, but of Nathan and others, who were not kings. (See genealogy page 97.) As Mary the wife of Joseph, was, according to Luke, the 42nd generation from David the king ; if Mary the wife of Cleophas, had been *her sister*, she also must have been 42 *generations distant from royalty*. If the grandsons of Judas, mentioned by Eusebius, had traced their lineage from David through *Mary*, they must been 45 *generations* removed from true royal blood! Yet those are the men whose relationship to the house of David alarmed Domitian as much as the appearing of Christ had Herod!

An Emperor of Rome would not have trembled with alarm, fearing as dangerous rivals, poor, hard handed, unambitious peasants of Galilee, who were 45 generation from the blood of a king! and then tracing their lineage through females for that! Females were not reckoned as links in a Hebrew genealogy. A title to a crown could not be inherited except by male descent. Jesus, though by his mother He was a descendant of David, yet was He the legal son and heir of David through Joseph, the lawful husband of his mother.

If James and Judas, the brothers of our Lord, had been related to "the son of David," King of the Jews, only because their *mothor* was sister to his *mother*, they would not have been considered or acknowledged by the Jews as heirs to the throne of David, and Domitian would never have been alarmed at such faint shadows of royalty, so dimly seen in the distance, through 45 generations, and traced through a female for that!

When Jesus the elder brother, was cut off, then the title of "king of the Jews" went to his brother, (and it meant something with a people who were looking for the Messiah, the son of David.) As Judas was *legally* the brother of Christ, being the son of Joseph, therefore Domitian feared his grandsons, as being of the blood royal of the house of David.

Perhaps some one, observing from the true table which 1 have constructed from Matthew, Luke and Eusebius, that a Judas was really of the royal house of David, through Cleophas, the brother of Joseph, may attempt to explain Domitian's fear of the family of Judas, because they were, through Cleophas, of royal blood. But let it be remembered, that the same authority which informs us that Cleophas was the brother of Joseph, calls the son of Cleophas, "cousin to our Saviour," (Eus. 1II. 11.) But the Judas who alarmed

Domitian, he says, was "*brother* to our Savior, according to the flesh." So that the Judas, whose descendants Domitian feared, was a *brother*, not a *cousin* of Christ—"a brother according to the flesh;" not according to a Hebrew idiom," a brother, as Greeks and Romans understood the word; such a brother to Christ as could be heir to Him.

The genealogical table which I have given from authentic sources, shows how all the persons connected with Christ, were related to Him, and each other; and will serve to illustrate this intricate portion of Scriptural and ecclesiastical history; and will make several subjects plain, which have been considered very confused, if not inexplicable.

If, for instance, we admit the theory that the two *Marys* were *sisters*, and Salome and her two sons no relation to Christ, it would be difficult to explain and defend the motive which emboldened Salome to make the singular request recorded in Matt. xx. 20. "Then came to Him the mother of Zebedee's children, with her sons, worshipping Him, and desiring a certain thing of Him. And He said unto her, "what wilt thou? She saith unto Him, grant that these my two sons may sit, the one on thy right hand, and the other on they left, in thy Kingdom."

To me this petition of Salome is perfectly intelligible, and consistent with the favorable character always given of the sons of Zebedee. Salome, being sister to the mother of Christ, her sons were the only Apostles related by blood to Him, and therefore, she concluded that they had the strongest claim to preferment; James and Judas, the sons of Cleophas, being *cousins* only in the eye of the law, their father being brother to Joseph. Salome's near relationship to Jesus, explains her reasons for presuming to prefer such a petition, consistently with her own pure character and the just rights of other disciples.

Though Christ did not reward John's devotion to Him by making him Minister of State, He conferred on him the highest proof of personal regard, when He said to his mother, "woman, behold thy son;" and to John, son, behold thy mother."

"From that hour that disciple took her to his own home," (John, xix, 27.)

John's mother Salome, appears to have retired with her sister from the cross, as was natural, to comfort her, now that a sword had pierced through her heart; for only the other two women were left to witness the burial. "Mary Magdalene and Mary the mother of Joses beheld where he was laid." (Mark. xv. 47.) "And there were Mary Magdalene, and the other Mary, sitting over against the Sepulchre," (Matt. xxvii. 61.) Then afterwards, "when the Sabbath was past, Mary Magdalene and Mary the mother of James, and *Salome* had bought sweet spices that they might anoint Him," (Mark. xvi. 1.)

How natural this is! Salome, having rendered all needful attentions to her bereaved sister, returns to the other women, to pay the last sad offices to her crucified Lord.

In all the incidents mentioned of Salome, from first to last, we see the devoted mother of John, and the affectionate sister of Mary, as well as the faithful follower of Christ. Such being the relationship of John to Jesus, their mothers being own sisters, and such being the preeminent fidelity of the disciple, whom Jesus loved and all three standing there by the cross, within hearing, with but one thought in their minds, and one feeling in their hearts, it is not unaccountable that our Lord should say to John, "son, behold thy mother." To whom else could He have spoken, when all others had forsaken Him, and fled?

We may charitably hope that James and Judas kept aloof in that day of peril, because their being brothers to the condemned "King of the Jews," exposed them to imminent danger. Whatever it was that kept them away, there was no other disciple but John, in that mourning group at the foot of the cross. No other had ventured near enough to receive a dying request from the lips of Him who was despised and rejected of men.

The hour of James was not yet come. He was reserved for other duties, and greater usefulness, in the future. The important part of his history begins where that of most of the apostles ends. Though he entered the vineyard of his labors at the eleventh hour, his after history, as developed in this book, proves that in this case, "the last became first." Whatever prominence was given to the other apostles the honor of being the first Bishop of Jerusalem, and of presiding in the first great council of the Church, was conceded to Him. (Eusebius, B. II. 1): "This James, who is termed the brother of the Lord, because he is called the son of Joseph * * this James, whom for his eminent virtues the ancients surnamed 'the Just,' was, as they relate, the first that had received the Episcopal seat of the Church at Jerusalem delivered unto him. So Clemens affirms in the 6th Book of his Institutions; for he says, that after the ascension of our Saviour, Peter, James, and John, although our Lord had preferred them before the rest, did not contend for the dignity, but chose James the Just bishop of Jerusalem. Paul makes mention of this James the Just, writing thus: "other of the Apostles saw I none, save James the Lord's brother."

Although this little work was originally designed to prove the existence of James the Lord's brother, and show who, and what, he was; yet, if what is here brought to light is truth, Bishop McIlvaine says correctly, "it upsets the whole Mariolatry of Rome, and all her claims to supremacy through Peter."

Some have asked, "what is *Mariolatry*?" Hook's Church Dictionary defines this word to mean, "worship of the Virgin Mary." Religions are sometimes named from the object worshipped. A religion which teaches men to pray and commit their all to Christ, is called *Christianity*; to an idol, *idolatry*; to Mary, *Mariolatry*. For example:

Acts, vii. 59. "Lord Jesus receive my spirit." That is *Christianity*.

First Kings, xviii. 26. "Oh, Baal, hear us," That is *Idolatry*.

Key of Heaven, page 50, "O Glorious Virgin Mary, I commit my soul and body to thy blessed trust this night, and forever, but more especially at the hour of my death. I recommend to thy merciful charity, all my hopes, my my consolations, my distress and my misery, my life and the end thereof, that through thy most holy intercession all my works may be directed, according to the will of thy blessed Son. Amen." That is *Mariolatry*.

COLLECT FOR THE THIRD SUNDAY IN ADVENT.

"O Lord Jesus Christ, who at thy first coming didst send thy messenger to prepare thy way before thee, grant that the ministers and stewards of thy mysteries may likewise so prepare and make ready thy way, by turning the hearts of the disobedient to the wisdom of the just, that, at thy second coming to judge the world, we may be found an acceptable people in thy sight, who livest and reignest with the Father, and the Holy Spirit, ever one God, world without end. Amen.

R. H. SIMPSON & CO., PRINTERS AND BINDERS.

www.ingramcontent.com/pod-product-compliance
Lightning Source LLC
LaVergne TN
LVHW021429110826
845150LV00007B/2145